Samsung Galaxy S24 Ultra (5G) Manual for Beginners and Seniors

A Complete User Guide with Tips and Tricks on How to Set up and use the New Samsung Galaxy S24 Ultra like a Pro.

Robert Jose

2

Table of Contents

Introduction

Within the pages of this user guide, you'll discover tips & tricks on how to set up and unlock the full potential of the new Samsung Galaxy S24 Ultra. As a beginner this user guide will boost your smartphone experience and make you a true professional of the new Galaxy S24 Ultra. This user guide comprises of numerous advanced feature of the new Galaxy S24 Ultra and it's the key to mastering every aspect of your device, ensuring that you make the most of its innovative features and powerful performance.

It's satisfactory for beginner and senior users.

Galaxy S24 Ultra layout

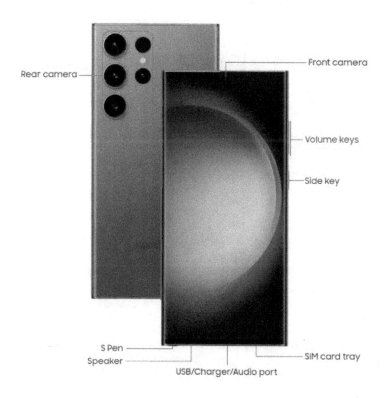

Rear camera

Front camera

Volume keys

Side key

S Pen
Speaker
USB/Charger/Audio port
SIM card tray

Chapter One
Set up the mobile device

The Galaxy S24 ultra uses Nano-SIM cards. You might be able to make use of your previous SIM card. The network accessibility of your model is the basis for network indicators for 5G service.

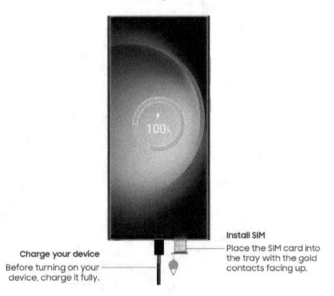

Install SIM
Place the SIM card into the tray with the gold contacts facing up.

Charge your device
Before turning on your device, charge it fully.

The Samsung S24 mobile device uses an IP68 rating for protecting water and dust. Do not allow water or dust to enter the tray hole and also ensure that the tray is properly placed into the hole before exposing it to liquids.

Maintaining water and dust resistance

Caution: To prevent electric shock and harm to your mobile device, do not charge it while it is wet. Do not use the smartphone, charger or cord with wet hands while charging.

It is essential that all compartment is closed tightly, otherwise the device will not be able to resist water and dust damage.

Comply with the following guidelines below to keep the mobile device functioning as it should in terms of water and dust.

- According to the IP68 standard of water resistant, that tests immersion in fresh water for periods that are longer than thirty minutes or deeper than meters of 1.5. Dry the device with a soft clean towel if it comes in contacts with fresh water or other liquid.

- Ensure the ports that can be opened are properly sealed to prevent water or other liquid substance from entering the device.

- You may not hear sound properly while making call due to damp microphone or speaker. Before using the device, wipe speaker and microphone part with a clean towel and then dry it.

- Exposing the device to water at high pressure may damage it.
- Have in mind that some certain features may not work if foreign objects get into the receiver, speaker or microphone. Always be mindful of where you keep the mobile device.
- The water and dust resistant feature may damage if the device receives hard impact.
- Do prevent unwanted noises during calls or media playback; do not cover the air vent hole with any accessory.

Charge the battery

Charge the device until it gets to 100% before using it for the first time.

NOTE: Do not use incompatible batteries, chargers and cables on your device, use only Samsung approved batteries, chargers and cables. Keep in mind that warranty doesn't cover damages cause by user misuse.

TIP: The device and charger may overheat and stop charging, it's normal, this usually does not affect the device's performance. Unplug the charge from the mobile device and wait a while for it to cool down.

Wireless power sharing

You can wirelessly share power between two devices that supports wireless power sharing feature. Take note that when wireless power sharing is activated, some feature may be unavailable.

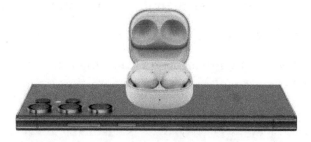

1. Unlock the device, launch settings app, select ⊚ Battery and device care > battery > Wireless power sharing.

2. Select battery limit and choose a percentage. Once you attain the estimated level of charge your device will end wireless power sharing automatically.

3. Activate this feature by tapping ◖ .

4. Position the device you want to charge on your phone back (as shown in the picture above). Your device will vibrate or make a sound when charging starts.

NOTE: The wireless power sharing feature is supported by majority of Qi-Certified Devices. This feature requires a minimum battery charge of thirty percent. Charging speed and efficiency of each device varies. Other manufacturer products such as coverings or attachment may not be compatible with the device. If connecting or charging a device is not working properly remove the cover from the device.

Start using your device

Press the Side key to switch on the Galaxy S24 ultra. When the device body is broken, do not use it until it has been fixed or repaired.

o Press the Side key to switch on the Galaxy S24 ultra.

- Tap ⏻ to switch the device off after pressing the Side Key and the Volume downward key.

- Tap ⏻ to restart the device after pressing the Side Key and the Volume downward key.

TIP: To know more about turning your device off;

Launch Setting app, select ⬚ Advanced features > Side key and then tap How to power off your phone.

NOTE: To use the 5G services properly, a strong 5G connection and unobstructed antenna is required. To know if the service is available consult your service provider.

Use the Setup Wizard

With the Setup Wizard, you can get a basic understanding on how-to setup the device when you power it on for the first time.

Kindly follow the instructions on the screen to choose language, create accounts, select location services, and connect Wi-Fi network.

Bring data from your old device

Get the Smart Switch application on Google Play Store or Galaxy Store to enable you move your Photos, Music, Contacts, Notes, Calendars, Videos, Messages, and more from your older device. You can also transfer data with Smart Switch using a computer, Wi-Fi, or a USB cable. For more information go to samsung.com/smart switch

1. Unlock the device and tap settings app, select
   Accounts and backup > Bring data from old device.

2. Kindly follow the instruction on the screen and select the items you want to transfer.

Lock and unlock

You can secure your device by using the screen lock features. By default, the phone screen will lock automatically when not in use or when the screen times out.

Side key
Press to lock.
Press to turn on the screen, and then swipe the screen to unlock it.

Side Key Setting

You can also change the Side Key's allocated shortcut.

Double press

Select a function to be launched when you press the Side Key twice.

1. Unlock the device and go to settings, tap 🔘 Advanced features then press Side Key.

2. Select **Double click** to activate this feature and then choose one of the following:

- Quick launch camera (default)
- Launch application

Push and hold

Select a feature to be activated when the Side Key is pushed and held.

1. Select 🔘 Advanced features > Side key under Settings.

2. Under the **press and hold** heading choose one of the following:

- Wake Bixby up
- Power off/ Shut down

Accounts

Create and manage your accounts.

Add a Google Account

Access your Google Cloud Storage, apps installed from your account, and Android features by logging into your Google Account

Signing into a Google Account and setting a lock screen activates Google Device Protection. When resetting to factory settings, you will need to provide your Google Account information.

1. Launch quick settings and tap ⟳ Accounts and backup > Manage accounts.

2. Tap ✛ to add account and then select Google.

Add a Samsung Account

To access exclusive Samsung content and use Samsung apps, sign in to your Samsung account.

- From the Settings page, select Samsung account.

Add an Outlook Account

View and manage your email messages by logging into your Outlook account.

1. From the Settings page, select ⟳ Accounts and backup > Manage accounts.

2. Tap ✚ to add account and then select Outlook.

Set up voicemail

Your voicemail services can be configured when you access it initially. It can also be accessed through the phone app.

1. To access voicemail from the 📞 phone app, launch the app and then tap 📧 or hold down the 1 1key.

2. Follow the guidelines on the screen to create a password, compose a greeting, and input your name.

Navigation

The best way to interact with a touch screen is to lightly press it with your finger. When excessive force is used on the touch screen or a metallic object is used on the screen, the surface may be damaged, and warranty coverage will be unavailable for that damage.

Tap

Launch or select items by touching them lightly.

- Using your finger, tap the item you want to select
- Click twice on an image to zoom in or out.

Swipe

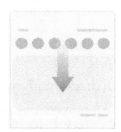

Swipe the screen lightly with your finger.

- You can unlock your device by swiping it
- Slide the screen to access the Home screen or menu options.

Drag and drop

Press and hold an object to change its position.

- To add an app shortcut to the Home screen drag it.
- Move a widget to a new position.

Zoom in and out

- Spread your finger as it is in the diagram above to zoom in.

- Bring your thumb and index finger together to zoom out.

Tap and hold

Press and hold an item to activate it.

- A menu option will pop up when you press and hold a field.

- Press and hold your Homes screen to change it settings and features.

Navigation Bar

A full screen gesture may be used to navigate your device if you do not want to use the navigation buttons.

Recent apps ———— ||| O < ———— Back

Home

Navigation buttons

To navigate quickly use the buttons at the bottom of the screen.

1. Launch settings, select  Display > Navigation bar > Buttons.

2. Select an option under Button order to decide where Back and Recent icons should appear on the screen.

Navigation gestures

Swipe to navigate your device instead of using the navigation buttons at the bottom of the screen.

1. Go to settings page, select Display > Navigation bar > Swipe gestures to make the feature active.

2. Tap any of the following options to modify it:

- More options: Select the kind of gesture and sensitivity.

- Gesture hint: Use lines to indicate the location of each screen gestures at the bottom of the screen.

- Switch apps when hint hidden: When gesture hint is off, you can use the gesture to turn between applications.

- Show button to hide keyboard: Hide the keyboard by displaying an icon in the bottom right corner of your screen, when your gadget is in portrait mode.

- Block gestures with S Pen: Make the S Pen unqualified of creating navigational gestures. This feature is only available on Samsung galaxy S24 Ultra only.

Customize your home screen

Your Samsung S24 ultra Home screen is the point whereby your screen navigation begins. There are more features than creating multiple Home screens, you can also delete screens, rearranges screens and also add your favorite apps and widgets.

App icons

Tap the application icon on the Home screen to open any app.

o Press and hold the icon of the app you want to move to the home screen and then tap ⊕ Add to Home.

To take out an icon:

While on the home screen, press and hold the icon of the app you want to remove and then tap 🗑 .

NOTE: When you remove an application icon from the home screen, it doesn't delete the app.

Wallpaper

Set your favorite image, preloaded wallpaper or video as wallpaper to change the appearance of your Home screen or Lock screen.

1. Press and hold any empty space in the home screen and then select 🖼 Wallpaper and style.

2. To view the list of available wallpapers, choose one of the menus listed below:

- Select photo to edit them on the Lock screen and home screen or your device.

- Change wallpapers: You can either download wallpapers from your Galaxy themes or select from the available ones.

- Color palette: You can select a palette based on colors from your wallpaper.

- Dim wallpaper when dark mode is on: Apply dark mode to make your wallpaper Make your wallpaper darker when it is on by applying dark mode.

Themes

You can decorate your Home screen, Lock screen, wallpapers, and app icons with a theme.

1. Click and hold the screen from your Home screen.

2. Click on ⛄ Themes to select a theme.

3. Click ☰ Menu > My stuff > Themes to view downloaded themes.

4. Select a theme and tap apply to activate it.

Icons

In order to replace the default icons, apply a different icon set.

1. Press and hold the screen while on the Home screen.

2. Click on ⛄ Themes > Icons to select an icon.

3. Click ☰ Menu > My stuff > Icons to view downloaded icons.

4. Select an icon and tap apply to activate it.

Widgets

To quickly access your data and apps, add a widget to the Home screen.

1. Touch and hold the screen while on your Home screen.

2. Press ⬤⬤ Widget and then select one.

3. Press Add on the widget you want to add to the Home screen.

Customize widgets

You can customize where and how a widget appears once you have added it.

o   While on the home screen, press and hold a widget and select any of the following option:

- ⊞ Create stack: Create a stack by adding more widgets of the same size in the same position on the Home screen.

- 🗑 Remove: Delete widget off your screen.

- ⚙ Settings: Change the widget's look or function.

- ⓘ App info: Access the permission, usage of widget, and other app info.

Home screen settings

1. Touch and hold the screen while on your Home screen.

2. To change the home screen settings, tap ⚙️ Settings:

- Home screen layout: Your device can be set to have different Home and Apps Screen or just one Home screen that all installed are located.

- Home screen grid: Select how icons appear on your phone screen by selecting a layout.

- Apps screen grid: Choose the pattern in which icons on the Apps screen are placed by selecting a layout.

- Folder grid: Choose a layout to decide how folders are being arranged.

- Add media page to Home screen: Swipe to the right to show a media page on your home screen after enabling this feature.

- Show Apps screen button on Home screen: For easy access to the Apps screen, add a button to the Home screen.

- Lock Home screen layout: Restrict the ability to move or remove items from the Home screen.

- Add new apps to Home screen: Home screen updates automatically when new apps are downloaded.

- Hide apps on Home and Apps screens: You can hide apps from the Home and App screens. Hidden apps are still installed and can appear in Finder searches.

- App icon badges: Choose the badge style for apps with active notifications.

- Swipe down for notification panel: You can open the Notification panel by swiping down anywhere on the Home screen if you enable this feature.

- Rotate to landscape mode: When you switch the orientation of your device from portrait to landscape, the Home screen rotates automatically.

Easy mode

In Easy mode, the text and icons are larger, making it easier to read. You can switch between the default screen layout and the simpler one.

1. To make easy mode active, go to settings, select Display > Easy mode and then tap to activate the feature.

2. The options below will pop up:

- Touch and hold delay: You can set the length of time it takes before a continuous touch is recognized.

- High contrast keyboard: High contrast colors are best for keyboards.

Status bar

Status icons

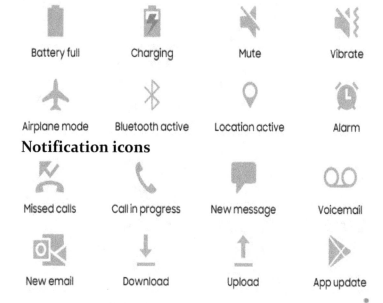

Battery full   Charging   Mute   Vibrate

Airplane mode   Bluetooth active   Location active   Alarm

Notification icons

Missed calls   Call in progress   New message   Voicemail

New email   Download   Upload   App update

TIP: To configure status bar notifications, press More options > Status bar in Quick settings.

Notification Panel

Pull down the notification panel to access notifications, settings and more.

Quick settings

Device settings

Notification cards

View the notification panel

The notification panel is easily accessible from any screen on your device.

1. Swipe your Screen downward to see the notification panel.

- Select an item to launch.

- Remove a single notification by dragging it to the left or right.

- Delete all your notification by touching clear.

- Customize your notification preferences by touching notification settings.

2. Swipe upward on your screen or press ‹ to close the notification panel.

Quick settings

The Notification panel offers quick access to device functions using the Quick Settings. Below are the most popular Quick settings. When you enable or disable an icon the color automatically changes.

1. Pull the status bar downward to show the notification panel.

2. Swipe down from the top of your screen once again to make Quick settings visible.

- Switch a Quick settings icon on or off by touching it.

- Press and hold the icon of the setting to open if quickly.

| Wi-Fi | Sound | Bluetooth | Auto rotate |

| Airplane mode | Location | Power saving | Dark mode |

Quick settings options

The following are included in the Quick Settings options.

- Search: Tap the search icon to find Apps or settings on your device.

- Power off: Tap the Power off icon to shut down or Restart the device.

- Settings: To quickly access the device's settings option, tap the Setting icon.

- More options: Customize the button layout.

- Device control: You can control other devices when you have an app like SmartThings or Google Home installed on your device.

- Media output: Control the playback of audio and video devices via the Media panel.

Chapter Two
S Pen

The S Pen offers useful functions, such as launching apps, taking notes, or drawing pictures. However, some S Pen functions, such as tapping the touchscreen, may not work near a magnet (only for Galaxy S24 Ultra).

S Pen button

Remove the S Pen

Your device's S Pen stores at the bottom for easy access and the pen can also be charged so that it can be used remotely.

o   Push the S Pen in and out to release it.

NOTE: In order to maintain the water-resistant and dust-resistant features of your device, keep the S Pen slot and opening free of dust and water, and ensure the pen is securely inserted before any liquid exposure.

Air view

To preview content or to view information about an item on the screen, hover the S Pen over it. Air view offers the following features:

- Preview and email before launching it.
- View a photo album or enlarge a picture
- Hover over the timeline to preview a video and navigate to a specific scene
- Find out what an icon or a button looks like by viewing its name or description

NOTE: Keep in mind that the preview features it only available when the S Pen's on-screen pointer is a solid color.

Air actions

The S Pen can be used for remote functions, such as opening apps, navigating screens, completing actions and more.

Only Samsung-approved S Pens with Bluetooth Low Energy (BLE) support the S Pen remote feature. If the S Pen is too far from the mobile device, you can't carry out the Air action when the S Pen is detached from the device.

   o Go to Settings page, select Advanced features > S Pen > Air actions to use the feature.

Hold the S Pen button shortcut

You can set a shortcut to launch the Camera app when you hold down the S Pen button.

1. Select Advanced feature > S Pen > Air actions from settings page.

2. Select Press and hold Pen button and the touch to activate the feature.

Anywhere action

The Anywhere actions can be accessed by holding the S Pen button while performing any of the following gestures: down, up, right, left, or shake. These can be used from any screen and can include navigation and S Pen features.

Action	Gesture
↶ Back	Left to right
⇄ Recents	Right to left
∿ Home	Up and down
� Smart select	Down and up
≋ Screen write	Zigzag

1. Select ⬚ Advanced features > S Pen > Air actions from the Settings.

2. Select a Gesture icon beneath Anywhere actions to change the shortcut.

App actions

In certain apps, you can use your S Pen to perform specific tasks.

1. Tap ⬚ Advanced features > S Pen > Air actions while in setting page.

2. Select an application to see the shortcuts available.

3. Click ⬤ to activate the shortcuts when using that application.

General app actions

Some basic actions can be customized when using camera and media apps not listed in the app action list.

1. Select ⬤ Advanced features > S Pen > Air actions from the Settings.

2. To change a specific action under General app action, touch it.

Screen off memo

The screen off memo setting must be enabled to allow you to write memos without turning on the screen. visit Configure S Pen settings for more info.

1. Take the S Pen off the device, and write on the screen.

2. Select an option to modify your memo:

   ▪ Color: Adjust the S Pen color

   ▪ ⬤ Pen settings: Double tap the Pen tool to alter the line thickness.

- ⬦ Eraser: Double tap the eraser tool to erase all.

3. Save your memo in your Samsung note app by tapping Save.

TIP: If the S pen has already been separated from the phone, tap the S pen button and press the screen to begin a note while the screen is off.

Pin to Always on display

The Always on Display can accommodate edited or pinned memos.

1. Select this ✐ icon to Pinto Always on Display from your screen-off note

2. Press Pin from the Always on Display Screen.

Air command

Access smart select, Samsung notes, and other capabilities of the S Pen from another screen

Settings

1. Select the ✐ Air command button or press and hold the S Pen close to the screen so that the pointer display.

2. Pick from the following alternatives:

- **Create notes:** Create new notes on the Samsung Note app.

- **View your notes:** From your Samsung Note app view all your created notes.

- **Smart select:** Add a portion of the display to the Gallery

- **Screenwriting:** Add text or arts on your screenshots

- **Live messages:** Draw or write a short-animated message with the S Pen.

- **AR Doodle:** Compose relative doodle with the capability of your galaxy S24 camera.

- **Translate:** Listen to the pronunciation of a word in another language by flipping the S Pen over the word.

- **PENUP:** Your S Pen is also capable of Creating, Editing, and Sharing of live drawing

- **Add:** Expand Air command apps and features menu selection.

- ⚙ Settings: Configure apps and features as well as the way menu is displayed to personalize Air Command.

Compose a note

Start composing a note in your Galaxy Note application.

- o Unlock the device and Select ✏ Air command and tap ➕ Create Notes.

View all notes

From your Galaxy Notes app, you can check all your created note.

- o Unlock the device and Select ✏ Air command > 📄 View all Notes.

Smart selects

Use the Smart select to copy any screen that can be shared with your contacts or added to your Gallery.

1. Unlock the device and ✏ Air command Menu > the select 🔲 Smart select.

2. Select a shape in the menu and drag the S Pen to select the content. The following options will appear:

- ⬜ Pin: Put a shortcut to the merged details in an application or on the Home screen of the Galaxy device.

- ⬜ Automatic selection: Grant the Smart select the permission of selecting contents to extract automatically.

- ✏️ Draw: Draw on your captured content.

- ⬜ Extract text: Find and locate texts from contents chosen.

- ⬘ Share: Select how your contents are to be distributed.

3. Select ⬇️ Save.

TIP: Press ⬜ to pin to a material to your screen to press ⬜ to record and animation using the Smart select.

56

Screen writes

Use the Screen write feature to draw or write text on your screenshots.

1. Unlock the Galaxy device and Select ⬤ Air command > 🔵 Screen Write.

2. After capturing the present screen, a pen tool will appear. The following available editing tools displays:

- Crop: Drag the edges of the screen to re-shape or resize the image that was captured.

- 🖋 Pen type: Use the pen type to draw on your screenshot. Alter the pen tip, color, and size by touching the pen symbol twice.

- ◇ Eraser: Clean annotations or writings off from your screenshots.

- ↶ Undo: Reverse the previous action

- ↷ Redo: Retake the recent action that was undone.

- ◁ Share: Determine how your contents are moved.

- ⦙Scroll capture: Record any scrollable portions of your screen that are hidden.

3. The Gallery app will store your contents after click ⬇ Save.

NOTE: To delete any drawing that you have made on the screen note Press and hold the S Pen button.

Live messages

Create a recorded animated drawing or written message.

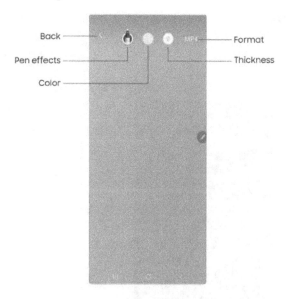

1. Open the device and go to 🖊 Air command > 💟 Live messages.

2. Select a background from the available choices:

- Collection: From your collections, you can view all your created live messages.

- Gallery: Select a background photo or video.

- Camera: Snap a background picture.

- Color: Determine the color of your background

3. Follow the on-screen instructions to begin creating your live messages

4. To save select Finish.

AR Doodle

Use the AR Doodle on faces or other items visible to the camera.

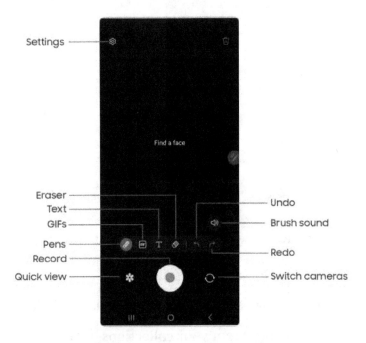

1. Select AR Doodle from the Air command menu on your Galaxy device

2. Switch between the front and back camera by touching Switch cameras.

3. To make sure that the center of the screen is where you want to shoot set up the camera

4. Draw a doodle with the S Pen.

- The doodle follows the face's motions in real time.

5. To record and save your AR Doodle as a movie click ⊛ .

Translate

To listen to pronunciation and translation of words use the S Pen to hover over words.

1. From the Apps screen, select 🖊 Air command > 🅰 Translate.

2. Touch the icon to select between translating a word translating phrase:

- Ⓣ Words: Translate a word completely

- ▤ Phrases: Translate a phrase completely.

3. To switch between languages, tap the source and target language.

4. Flip the S Pen over a word.

- To hear a word in the source language press ◁))) Sound.

- To add the translated texts and texts that are recently selected to clipboard select ⬜ Copy.

5. To cancel the translation, click ✕ .

PENUP

Use the Galaxy S24 S Pen to Edit, Color, Draw and share live drawings.

o Launch the ● Air command menu > tap 🔺 PENUP on your smart device.

Add shortcut

Air command menu can be edited by adding shortcuts to apps and functions.

1. Select ⊕ Add under ● Air command on your Smart Phone.

2. Select apps and function that you would prefer to add to the Air Command menu.

- To eliminate and app shortcut click on ⊖ .

3. Save your selection by selecting 〈.

Air command settings

Utilize a suitable menu that you can move to any part of your screen to access S Pen functions and apps quickly.

- o Unlock the device and select ⚙ Advanced from Settings and then press S Pen > Air command to customize the followings:
- ▪ Menu style: Choose a menu to display when you launch the Air command menu
- ▪ Shortcuts: Choose the shortcut that you can access on the Air Command.
- ▪ Show Air Command icon: Set the mobile device to show a button for the Air command option.
- ▪ Open the Air Command menu with the S Pen button: Use the S Pen button to launch Air command.

Configure S Pen settings

The setting of the S Pen can be changed. Each service provider with their own options.

o Select ⚙ Advanced features > S Pen from Settings to set up the following options.

- Air Action: Configure the remote control's behavior while using apps with.

- Air Command: Set the shortcuts, style, and functionality of the Air command menu.

- Air view: You can turn the Air view off.

- S Pen to text: You can use the S Pen to write in search fields.

- When S Pen is separated from the device: You can determine what happens either to Launch Air Command or create a note.

- Screen off memos: Remove your S Pen to create Screen off memos by removing the when the screen is off and writing on the screen afterwards. Screen off memos are stored in your Samsung Notes app.

- Quick notes: To create a new note, tap the screen with the S Pen twice after pressing and holding the S Pen button.

- More S Pen settings: Your S Pen can be set to carry out additional actions by setting connections, noise, and vibrations.

Chapter Three
Bixby

This feature learns changes and adapt to your pattern. It assists you in setting up reminders after being familiar with your routines depending on the time, place and is integrated into you selected apps. Go to Samsung.com/us/support/owner/app/Bixby, for more information.

o Press and hold the Side key when on a Home screen.

TIP: The Apps list is another way to go to Bixby.

Bixby vision

Bixby vision is linked with your camera, Gallery and internet apps to help you understand what you see better. It features includes contextual icons for purchasing, QR code detection, landmark recognition and translation.

Camera

You can access Bixby on the camera view finder to get a better understanding of what you see. Select Bixby Vision under More from the camera app.

Gallery

You can use Bixby on images and videos saved on you Gallery application.

1. Select an image to view in the ✱ Gallery app.

2. Click 👁 Bixby vision.

Internet

The Bixby Vision can be used to know more about a photo in the internet app.

1. Press and hold a specific photo on the 🔘 internet app to launch a pop-up menu.

2. Select search with Bixby.

Modes and Routines

Configure your device settings to automatically adjust based on your vicinity or activity by composing modes and routines.

o Choose 🔘 Modes and Routines for the preview of the following pages:

- Modes: Choose a Mode based on your location and your present activity.

- Routines: Create pattern for calls based on your current location or the time.

Digital wellbeing and parental controls

Digital habits can be monitored and controlled by you keeping track of the number of times your phone applications are being used, the number of alerts received, and how often your device is being checked daily. You can configure your device to help you wind down automatically before sleeping.

○ Press Digital Wellbeing and Parental Control in the Settings menu for the following features:

▪ Click on the dashboard to access the following;

− Screen times: View the number of times and application used every day.

− Alerts received: View the number of notifications an app has received that day.

− Times Unlocked: View the statistics of your app daily usage.

▪ Screen time: View your daily standard by setting up a screen time objective.

- App timers: Restrict your usage of an app each day.

- Driving monitor: Use your vehicle Bluetooth to check which app you mostly make use of to monitor your screen time while driving.

- Volume monitor: Protect your hearing by selecting a sound source to watch over the volume.

- Parental controls: Monitor the digital life of your kids with the Google Family Link app. You can select apps, create content filters, control your screen usage, and compel screen time limitations.

Always On Display

With the Always on Display time, date, missed calls, messages, notifications, and other customized data can be checked without unlocking the device.

1. Unlock the device and select ⬛ Lock screen > Always on Display under the Settings menu.

2. Choose the following settings after clicking 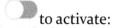 to activate:

- You can choose whether you want your clock and notifications to display when the smart phone is not in use.

- Clock style: You can change the color and style of your clock both on the Always on Display screen or your Lock Screen

- Show music information: The information of a music will appear when you activate the Face Widget music controller.

- Screen orientation: Your AOD can appear either in landscape or portrait mode.

- Automatic brightness: You can adjust the brightness of the AOD automatically.

Always on Display Themes

1. Unlock your gadget and select Always on Display from ⊓ Themes menu on your Home Screen by pressing and holding the screen.

- Select AOD to preview and download to My Always on Display.

2. Select AOD from my Stuff under ☰ Menu to see your themes that have been downloaded.

3. Select the Always On Display and click on apply.

Biometric security

Secure your device and login to your accounts using biometric security.

Recognition of Face

Unlock your device after activating Face Unlock. A PIN, Pattern, or Password must be set up to use this feature.

- The security of your face is less secured than that of a Password, Pin, or Pattern. If you are using this face recognition someone or something like your image can be used to unlock the device.

- Face recognition process may be interrupted if you are using heavy make-ups, beards, hats, glasses.

- Ensure you are in a well lightened area and clean up your camera lens properly before enrolling your face.

1. Unlock your mobile device, go to Settings > ⬤ Security & privacy > Biometrics and then tap Face recognition.

2. Follow the face recognition instructions.

Face Recognition Management

Customize your face recognition.

○ To access Face recognition, select Settings > ⬤ Security and privacy > Biometrics.

- Remove face data: Get rid of existing faces.

- Upload different appearance to enhance face recognition.

- You can use the face unlock to activate or deactivate device security.

- Remain on the Lock screen until you swipe the screen when you are using face recognition.

- Your face will be identified only when your eyes are opened.

- Make your face easier to recognize in low light condition by increasing your screen brightness temporarily.

- Learn more on how to protect your device using face recognition.

Fingerprint Scanner

Instead of typing your password in some apps you can use your fingerprint. Your fingerprint can also be used to verify your identity when logging in to your Samsung account. To set up the fingerprint unlock your device must have a PIN, Password, or Pattern.

1. Unlock your mobile device and launch Settings > Security and privacy > Biometrics > Fingerprints.

2. Follow the fingerprint registration process to enroll your fingerprint.

Fingerprint Management

Fingerprints can be added, removed, or renamed.

- ○ Unlock your gadget and go to Settings > Security and privacy > Biometrics > Fingerprints to access the options below:

- The list of fingerprints registered will appear first on the list. Select a fingerprint to either delete it or rename it.

- Follow the instruction to add up another fingerprint.

- Confirm additional fingerprints: Scan your fingerprint to check if it has been successfully added.

Fingerprint Validation Settings

Validate your identity in apps and actions that are compatible using the fingerprint recognition.

1. Unlock the mobile device and launch Settings > Security and privacy > Biometrics > Fingerprints.

- Unlock with fingerprint: use your fingerprint as a process of authentication to unlock your device.

- You can also scan your fingerprint even when your screen is off.

- Fingerprint icon will appear even when your screen is off.

- Show animation when unlocking your device using the fingerprint authentication.

Settings for Biometric

Set up your selections for biometric security measures that are available.

o Unlock your Smart Phone and select Settings > Security and privacy > Biometrics for the following options:

▪ Show unlock transition effects: Employ a transitional effect when you unlock your device with biometric.

Edge panels

Several customizable panels that make up the Edge panel can be accessed from the edge of the screen. News, sport, and other information as well as apps, tasks and contacts can be viewed with the Edge panel.

o Unlock the device and launch Settings > Display > Edge panels then press to activate the feature.

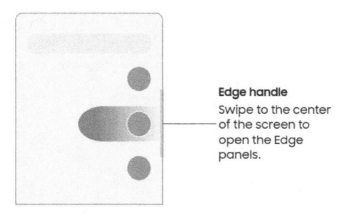

Edge handle
Swipe to the center of the screen to open the Edge panels.

Application panel

An add app button is included in the app section.

1. From any screen drag the Edge Handle to the center of the screen. Swipe upward with your finger to display the Apps panel.

2. To launch and app shortcut select the app or pair of apps. You can click ⋮⋮ All apps for the full list of apps to display.

3. To launch additional windows in the pop-up window, drag the app icon from the Apps panel.

How to set up the Apps panel:

1. Personalize the Apps panel by dragging the Edge Handle to the middle of your screen from any screen. Swipe upward to display the Apps panel.

2. To upload other apps in the Apps panel select Edit ✎ .

- On the left side of the screen you will find the app you want to upload to the Apps panel, move it to an empty space in the right column.

- You can create another folder shortcut for an app by dragging the app from the left-hand side of the screen to the right-hand column.

- When you want to adjust the order of the apps in the folder drag the app to the location you want it to be on the panel.

- When you want to uninstall the app select ⬛ Remove.

3. When you want to save your changes select ＜ .

Personalize Edge Panels

You can personalize each Edge panel.

1. Unlock the mobile device and enter Settings > ⚙ Display > Edge panels > Panels.

2. The following alternatives will show

- ✅ Checkbox: With this you can turn panel on or off.

- Edit: Configure personal/individual panels.

- 🔍 Search: Search for panels that already installed or available for installation.

- ⋮ More options:

- Re-position: Drag panels to the right or left to position them in separate sequence.

- Uninstall: Delete an Edge panel that was downloaded on your device.

- Hide on Lock screen: Pick which panel to hide on the lock screen when you set up a secure screen lock.

▪ Galaxy Store: From the Galaxy Store you can download more edge panels.

3. Tap ⟨ to save your changes.

Position and Style of the Edge Panel

You can personalize the position of the Edge handle.

○ Unlock the mobile device and select settings > ⊙ Display > Edge panels > Handle for the following options:

▪ Edge handle: Change the placement of the Edge handle in accordance with the screen edge.

▪ Position: Choose either right or left to indicate the position in which the Edge screen appears.

▪ Lock handle position: Activating this feature will enable the handle position from shifting when you touch it.

▪ Style: Select a color and style for the Edge handle.

- Transparency: Change the Edge handle transparency with the transparency slider.

- Size: Drag this slider to adjust the size of the Edge handle.

- Width: Drag this slider to adjust the width of the Edge handle.

- React to touch by vibration: When you touch the Edge handle it will vibrate.

About the Edge panels

Check the features software version and license information of the Edge panel.

o Enter the Settings app and tap Display > Edge panels > About Edge panels.

Enter Text

When using Samsung keyboard, you can enter text by typing it or using the voice input feature.

Expand toolbar

Toolbar

You can use the toolbar to access your keyboard function quickly.

o You can access the following by selecting expand toolbar on the Samsung keyboard:

▪ ☺ Expression: Explore varieties of emoji, GIFs, and create special emoji combination and more.

- Clipboard: Access to the clipboard.

- One-handed keyboard: Change your keyboard layout to a one-handed mode.

- Voice input: Use your Samsung device voice input.

- Settings: Access the keyboard's settings.

- Handwriting: When using Galaxy S24 ultra, this feature is available.

- Split keyboard: Change to a share keyboard that is divided.

- Floating keyboard: Your keyboard can be repositioned wherever you want on the screen if you make it floating.

- Search: Use the Search feature to look for words or phrases in conversations.

- Translate: Use your Samsung keyboard to translate typed words into another language.

- ⊤ Extract text: Copy texts from the selected contents.

- Samsung Pass: Use biometrics to easily access your personal data and online accounts with the Samsung Pass.

- Ⓖ Grammarly: This feature will suggest word as you type.

- Emoji: Upload an emoji.

- GIFs: Upload moving GIFs.

- Bitmoji: Customize your own emoji to use as stickers.

- Mojitok: Select from available stickers or create your own.

- AR Emoji: Use your edited emoji as stickers.

- Spotify: Upload Spotify music.

- YouTube: Upload YouTube videos

- Size of your keyboard: Change the height and width of your keyboard.

- ◌ Text editing: Use an editing panel to help you find texts to cut, copy, and paste.

Personalize the Samsung Keyboard

Personalize setting for the Samsung keyboard.

- o On the keyboard select ⚙ settings to access the following alternatives:

- ▪ Languages types: Select the languages that can be typed in the keyboard.

- – Switch between languages by swiping to the right on the space bar.

Smart typing

- ▪ Predictive texts: As you type you will see suggested words and phrase.

- ▪ Suggested emoji: Upload emoji when using predictive texts.

- ▪ Suggest stickers while typing: As you type suggested stickers will appear.

- ▪ Automatic replace: Automatically replace what you type using predictive texts suggestion.

- Suggest text correction: Misspelled words are underline in red and correction will appear on the keyboard.

- Text shortcuts: Establish shortcuts expressions that are regularly used.

- Additional typing alternatives: Upload more customized options.

Layout and Style

- Keyboard toolbar: The keyboard toolbar can be shown or hidden.

- High contrast keyboard: Change the color and size of your Galaxy S24 ultra keyboard to enhance the contrast between the keys and the background.

- Theme: Select a keyboard theme design.

- Mode: Select an orientation either landscape or portrait.

- Transparency and size: Personalize the transparency and size of your keyboard.

- Keyboard Layout: Display unique characters and digits on the keyboard.

- Font size: Move the slider to personalize the font size.

- Custom symbols: Customize the keyboard's shortcut for symbols.

Other settings

- Voice input: Set up voice input services and preferences.

- Swipe, touch, and feedback: Change feedback and movements.

- Handwriting: You can customize handwriting options on the keyboard.

- Text with S Pen: Write on search bars and address bars with the S Pen. Galaxy S24 ultra will transform your handwriting into texts.

- Save screenshot to clipboard: Activate saving screenshots to the clipboard on the keyboard.

- Select third party contents to use: Activate the features for the Third-party keyboard.

- Reset to default: Reset your keyboard to the normal settings and delete all personalized data.

- Details about Samsung keyboard: See Samsung keyboard legal details and version.
- Contact Samsung support through Samsung members.

Chapter Four
Camera & Gallery

Capture videos and pictures of high quality with the Camera app. View and personalize your pictures and videos on the Gallery app where they are stored.

Camera

Use the full package of professional lenses and advanced video settings.

- Unlock the mobile device and select  Camera on the Apps list.

TIP: Double click the side key to launch the Camera app quickly.

Settings

Zoom

Shooting modes

Switch cameras

Gallery

Capture

Navigate the camera screen

With the front and back cameras, you can capture beautiful selfie or picture.

1. Launch the camera application, and set up your shot using the option beneath:

- Touch the screen in the position you want the camera to focus on.

- The Galaxy S24 ultra screen displays a brightness scale if you click it. To alter the brightness level, drag the slider.

- Move the device screen upward and downward to speedily switch between the front and back cameras.

- To zoom in accurately, hit (1x) at the lower end options on the screen (This feature is only available if the rear camera is in use.)

- Use the tip of your finger to swipe the screen right or left to adjust between shooting modes.

- To change camera settings, go to ⚙ settings.

2. Select ⭕ Capture.

Set up the shooting mode

To capture a picture, you can either allow the camera to select a shooting mode or choose from the range of the shooting modes provided. While on the camera app, use the tip of your finger to swipe the screen right or left to adjust between shooting modes.

- Portrait: Portrait feature blurs the background when capturing picture.

- Allow camera to select the finest settings when taking pictures.

- Video: When shooting videos, allow the camera to choose the finest settings for the video.

- Additional: To add or delete shooting mode from the options displayed at the bottom of the camera screen, select Add.

- Expert RAW: The expert RAW shooting mode should be saved to your computer.

- Pro: The exposure setting, color, ISO sensitivity and white balance can be adjusted manually while taking pictures.

- Pro video: You can manually alter the exposure value, ISO sensitivity, color and white balance when shooting videos in high quality.

- Single-take photography and filming: Take a number of pictures and videos from diverse perspectives.

- Panoramic: To create linear photos, take snapshots either vertically or horizontally.

- Night: You can use the device to take images in faint light without the use of flash.

- Food: create photographs that highlight the vibrant colors of the food.

- Super slow motion: You can shoot videos in extremely high super slow mo and watch a specific section.

- Hyper lapse: Make a time lapse video by capture quite a few frames per second recordings. The frame rate can be adjusted depending on the scene being captured.

- Portrait video: The background will blur when shooting portrait movie or pictures.

AR Zone

Open all of your augmented reality features from one place. Click More on the Camera app and click AR Zone. The features below are accessible:

- Augmented Reality Emoji Studio: Work with the tools of the AR to create and customize your own emoji.

- Augmented Reality Emoji Camera: Use the camera app to make you own emoji avatar.

- Augmented Reality Stickers: Including stickers of the AR emoji to my Emoji avatar.

- Augmented Reality Doodle: to improve videos include drawn lines or handwriting to your environment. Your movement is being followed by the AR Doodle by tracking your faces and space

- Deco Pic: In real time add design to images or movies with the camera.

- Quick measure: Measure objects in inches or millimeters on your camera using the Quick measurement feature.

Space Zoom

Capture accurate photos at magnification of up to 100 times (only available on Samsung Galaxy S24 Ultra).

1. Select a level of magnification by touching the shortcut for zoom under Camera.

- Center you photo on the frame then select ⅔〰⅔

  Zoom lock to receive actual zoom focusing while taking photos at a higher magnification.

2. Select ◯ to take a photo.

Recording videos

With your Samsung S24 device, you can create vivid videos.

1. Swipe left or right on your screen to alternate between the camera and video mode

- Press the Record button to start shooting a video.

- Press ⊙ to capture a photo while recording a video.

- Hit the pause button ‖ to temporarily end recording. To resume recording, press ● .

2. To end recording click the Stop button ■ .

Recording 360 audio

With the 360-audio recording feature, you can record immersive 3D sound with Bluetooth headphones.

1. On the 📷 Camera screen, click ⚙️ Settings.

2. Click 360 audio recording from Advanced option menu to activate this feature.

Settings for the Camera

Utilize the settings options and icons on the main camera screen to set up your camera.

o On the 📷 Camera screen, select ⚙️ Settings to launch the following options:

Intelligent features

- Scene optimizer: Make your photo color settings adapt to the scene automatically.

- Shot suggestions: To capture perfect shot follow the on-screen instructions.

- Scan QR codes: When using the camera, the device will detect QR codes automatically.

Pictures

- You can determine either to shoot a burst shot or create a GIF when you swipe the shutter button to the edge.

- Watermark: Place a watermark at the bottom left corner of your image

- Additional pictures options: Choosing file formats and additional saving options.

- High efficiency photos: Store your images as a high efficiency format to conserve space. Not all sharing websites supports the format.

- Pro mode photo format: Determine the format to save Pro mode photos.

Selfies

- Save selfies as preview: Save Selfies the way they appear in the preview screen without flipping them.

Videos

- Auto FPS: The Auto FPS feature optimizes the frame the frame rate of recording brighter videos in lowlight in the video mode.

- Video stabilization: Activate Anti-shake to maintain the focus when moving the camera for stabilization of your video.

- More video options: Enhance your recordings using the cutting-edge recording format.

  - High efficiency Videos: Record your videos in HEVC format to conserve storage space. Not all phone or websites support the playback format.

  - Professional videos with high bitrates: Utilize the Pro video shooting option to capture videos at a higher bit rate.

  - HDR10+ movies: Capture HDR+10 recordings to improve videos. Playback devices need to support HDR+10 videos.

  - Microphone Zoom-in: Link the mic zoom with the camera zoom while recording videos.

  - Recording 360 audio: Record 3D lifelike and realistic audio using you Bluetooth headphone.

General

- Auto-Focus Tracking: Concentrate on a moving object.

- Gridlines: Show viewfinder gridlines to enhance composition of images or videos.
- Location tags: Allocate a GPS location tag to your picture or video
- Methods for shooting:
  - Use the Volume keys to zoom, record videos, adjust volume and take pictures, by pressing it.
  - Voice command: When photo is been capture speak important phrase.
  - Floating shutter button: Add another shutter that you can place on any part of the screen.
  - Display palm: Hold your hands while your palm is facing the camera to capture a picture quickly.
- Setting to keep: Decide to open Camera with the same shooting mode, selfie angle, and filters as the recent launch.
- Shutter sound: Produce a sound while taking photos.
- Vibration feedback: Press the screen to activate vibration feedback.

Privacy

- Privacy notice: Check the privacy policy of Samsung.

- Permission: you can view the necessary optional camera app permission.

Others

- Reset setting: Restore the Camera preferences to default.

- Contact us at: Ask for help from Samsung through Samsung members.

Gallery

Launch gallery application to see all the visible items saved to your device. From the Gallery application, you can view edit and manage images and videos.

o Open the device and select ✲ Gallery from the application screen.

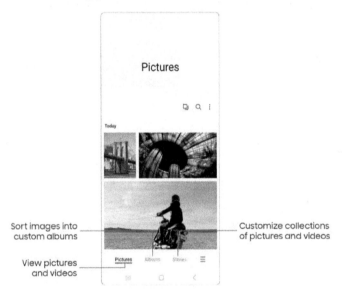

Sort images into custom albums

View pictures and videos

Customize collections of pictures and videos

View images

You can view your device images using the gallery app

1. Launch the ✲ Gallery application from the apps screen and select a picture.

100

2. Select the picture you want to view and then swipe right or left to see more.

- To enable Bixby for photos, click ⊙ Bixby.

- To add photo to the favorite list, click ♡ Favorites

- To use the following features, click ⋮ More options:

- Details: View and change data associated with an image

- Remaster photo: Use automatics image enhancements to refine a picture.

- Add portrait effect: The background visibility in your portrait photographs can be increased or decreased by dragging the slider

- Clipboard: Images can be copied to the clipboard to paste in another app.

- Set image as wallpaper: Use the image as a background on your desktop.

- Secure folder: Click on the secure folder button to move the image to a secure folder.

- Print: Send the image to a nearby printer for printing.

Edit pictures

Use the editing tools to improve your pictures quality.

1. From the application screen, launch ✳ Gallery and tap a Picture.

2. Press ✎ Edit for the following options after selecting the picture:

- ☀ Auto change: Make changes to enhance your image automatically

- ⊡ Convert: Rotate, flip, crop, or make other changes to the overall appearance of the image.

- ◑ Filters: Adjust the color effects.

- ☼ Tone: Adjust spotlight, intensity contrast and other tone aspects

- ☺ : Decorate your photos with texts, stickers or hand-drawn contents.

- ⋮ : From more options use additional editing features.

- Revert: Go back to the original quality of the image.

3. To save changes, Click **Save.**

Play video

Watch and view videos details. You can add your best videos to favorites list.

1. Unlock your gadget and select a video from ✳ Gallery application.

2. Click a video to watch. Use your finger tip to slide right or left to see more.

- If you wish to add a video to your favorites list, click ♡ Add to favorites.

- To use the following features, click on ⋮ More option:

- Details: You can check and change the video info.

- Open in video player: View videos with the in-built video player.

103

- Wallpaper: Use the video as a background on the lock screen.
- Secure folder: Click the secure folder button to add the video to the secure folder.

3. To watch the video, click ▶ play.

Video brightness

Enhance the quality of the images in your video to enjoy a brighter color.

o From the Settings application, hit ⚙ Advanced > Video brightness and then select the option you want to apply.

Edit Video

Arrange and personalize your device videos.

1. From ✳ Gallery application from the apps screen and select a Picture.

2. Click on a video to watch.

3. Tapping ✎ Edit can enable you gain access to the following tools:

▪ 🔊 Audio: Adjust the level of loudness and video background music.

- ✂ Trim: Cut a segment of the video.

- ⟳ Transform: Change: Rotate, Crop, or Flip to change the video overall appearance.

- ◷ Filters: Use visible effects to enhance your videos.

- ☼ Tone: Adjust Brightness, Contrast and exposure of the video.

- ☺ Decorations: Decorate your video with texts of hand-drawn contents.

- ⋮ More options: For more option use additional editing features.

- Revert: Alter the changes made to return your video to its original quality

4. To save changes, press Save.

Share pictures and videos

From the Gallery, you can share images and videos

1. From the ✳ Gallery application, click a picture.

105

2. Click ⋮ More options > Edit after selecting videos and images to be shared.

3. To share selected items, click ⬳ share and choose the app you want to use in sharing them and follow the guidelines.

Delete images and videos

If you want to delete an image or video, you can do so from the Gallery application.

1. Unlock your Smartphone and select ✳ Gallery > ⋮ More options > Edit.

2. Pick images and videos to be deleted.

3. Click 🗑 Delete.

Group comparable images

Images and videos can be grouped based on their similarity

1. From ✳ Gallery, press ▱ Group similar photo.

2. To return to the default display of your Gallery, select ▱ Ungroup.

Screenshot

Capture a screenshot. On your Gallery app a folder for screenshot will be created automatically on your Smartphone.

o To capture a screenshot from any screen press and hold the side key and the volume downward key together.

Palm swipe to capture a screenshot

To capture a screenshot with this feature swipe the edge of your hand across the screen still maintaining contact with the screen

1. Launch the Settings app and click Palm Swipe to capture under Advanced features.

2. To activate this feature, press .

Screenshot settings

Personalize your Screenshot.

o From settings page, click Advanced features > Screenshot and Screen recorder.

▪ Show toolbar after capturing: After capturing a screenshot display more options.

- Delete after sharing from toolbar: After sharing screenshot from the screenshot toolbar delete them instantly.

- Hide the status bar and Navigation bar: Capture screenshot without the status bar and navigation bar appearing.

- Format: You can decide to save your screenshots as JPG or PNG files.

- Save screenshots: Select a location or folder to save your screenshot.

Screen recorder

Use screen record feature to record activities going on in your device, you can write notes, record videos of yourself and transfer them to your loved ones.

1. From the Quick settings menu, click   Screen recorder.

2. Click start recording after select silent or voiced screen recording.

3. Device will commence a three seconds countdown before the recording begins. To

begin immediate recording click skip countdown

- : Use the Draw tool to draw on your screen

- Tap Pointer to display an icon on the screen when you are using your S Pen (This feature only works on Samsung Galaxy S24 Ultra).

- To include a recording from your front camera, click Selfie video.

4. Use the Stop button to abort recording. The recording will be saved to a screen recording album on your Gallery app.

Screen recorder Settings

To adjust the screen recorder sound and quality settings, Launch the settings app and click Screenshot and Screen recorder under Advanced features.

- Sound: Select sound to be recorded while using the Screen recorder.

109

- Video quality: Determine a video quality resolution. You need more storage to use a higher resolution with better quality.
- Selfie video size: Use the slider to adjust the video overlay size.
- Display taps: Enable this feature to record tap on your screen.
- Save record: Select a location or folder you want to save you Screen recorded video.

Applications & Usage

The Apps list displays all downloaded and preinstalled applications. Users can download apps via Google Play Store or Galaxy Store.

o To launch the Apps list swipe the screen upward from the Home screen.

Deactivate or Delete applications

You can delete apps that are downloaded while preinstalled apps (available by default) can only be disabled. Disabled apps will be hidden from the apps screen

o To uninstall or disable an app from the Apps list press and hold the app and click Uninstall/Disable.

Search for Application

If you are finding it difficult to locate a particular app use the search feature.

1. Input one or more words in the search field at the top of your Apps list. As words are being typed apps and settings that match your search will appear.

2. Click on your desired result to launch the app.

TIP: To personalize the search settings, select ⠿ More options > Settings

Sort applications

You can decide to sort your apps alphabetically or in a custom order.

o On the Apps list, click ⠿ More options and tap Sort for the following options:

▪ Customize order: Arrange apps in a specific sequence manually.

▪ Alphabetical order: Arrange apps in an alphabetical order.

TIP: When apps are manually arranged empty icon spaces can be removed by clicking ⠿ More options > Clean up pages.

Create and use folders

From your Apps list you can make folders to sort app shortcut.

1. From Apps press and hold an application shortcut then pull it over another application until it is highlighted.

2. Click on the App shortcut to make a folder

- Create & Name Folder: Allocate a name to the folder.

- ◯ Palette: Change the folder color.

- ╪ Insert apps: Upload apps into the folder. Touch the app you want to add and tap Done.

3. Use the ‹ Back icon to close the folder.

Copy a folder to a Home screen

You can copy a folder to your device home screen

- ○ Select ⊕ Add to home after pressing and holding the folder.

Deleting a folder

Once you delete a folder app that were in the folder will appear on the Apps list.

1. Press and hold the folder you want to delete

2. Choose 🗑 Delete and adhere to when prompted.

Game Booster

You can get enhanced performance while you are playing games based on your usage. Deactivate notifications and turn on this feature to improve experience in Gaming.

- o To see the navigation bar when playing games, swipe upward from the bottom of your screen. The options below are available on the right and left sides:

- ▪ Touch protections: With the Touch Security enabled you can lock the screen to stop unauthorized taps.

- ▪ Game Booster: With the Game Booster activate you can set up additional options, such as blocking screenshots, the menu bar, and screen touches, as well as performance monitoring.

Application settings

Manage your downloaded applications.

- o Go to Settings page and press ⊞ Apps. Pick an option to change:

- Select default applications: By setting default apps you can select the apps to be used for calling, messaging, visiting websites, and more.

- Samsung application settings: You can change Samsung apps settings by viewing a list of apps.

- Your application: Click on an application to examine and make changes to its privacy and usage settings. All apps have their separate options.

TIP: Click Reset app preferences under ⋮ More options to return the app to its previous setting.

Calendar

You can connect the calendar application to various accounts online to put all your calendars in one place.

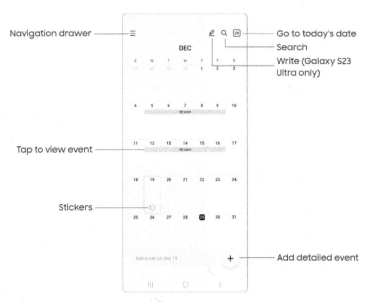

Navigation drawer
Go to today's date
Search
Write (Galaxy S23 Ultra only)
Tap to view event
Stickers
Add detailed event

Add calendars

From the Calendar app, you can create accounts.

1. Launch the Calendar application and click Navigation drawer.

2. Click ╀ Add account under Manage calendars and select an account format.

3. Enter details of the account and follow the on-screen guidelines.

TIP: Contacts and Emails can also be included in the accounts.

Calendar notifications style

From the Calendar application, you can select different types of notifications.

1. Launch the 🔘 Calendar application and click on ☰ Navigation drawer > ⚙️ Settings then tap Alert/Notification Style

   The following options will display:

- Light: Receive a notification when you hear a short sound.

- Medium: Receive a full screen notification when you hear a short sound.

- Strong: Get a full-screen notification and a ringing sound that is ongoing until it is dismissed.

2. The below choices will appear depending on the previous alert style selected:

- Brief sound: Choose the Light or Medium notification styles' alert sound.

- Long sound: Select the alert sound for the strong alert type.

Create Events

Utile your Calendar application to set up events.

1. Unlock the device and click 🔲 Calendars > ✚ Add detailed events to add an event.

2. Enter the details of the event and select Save.

Delete Events

From the Calendar app, Events can be deleted.

1. To change an event in the calendar app click it twice.

2. Press the 🗑 Delete button to remove an event.

Clock

With the clock app, you can track time and configure alarms.

Alarm

Using the alarm tab can enable you create a one-time frequent alarm and choose settings for notification.

1. From the ⊙ clock application menu on your Smartphone, select ┼ Add alarm.

2. Use the options listed as follows to set up an alarm:

-   Time: Chose a specific alarm time.

-   Day: Choose a specific day the alarm should ring.

-   Alarm name: Allocate a name to your alarm.

-   Alarm sound: Use the volume slider to change the volume level after choosing an alarm sound.

-   Vibration: You can decide that your alarm should vibrate as a reminder.

-   Snooze: Allow sleeping. While you are asleep set the space and number of times the alarm should be repeated.

3. To start using the alarm click Save.

TIP: To set up your bedtime reminder and automatically put the smartphone in Sleep mode, press ⋮ more options > Set Sleep mode schedule.

Deleting alarms

You can delete a created alarm.

o   From your Smartphone clock app press and hold an alarm and press 🗑 Delete.

Alert settings

Your Smartphone can be set to vibrate for alarms and timers, whether the mode of sound is set to Vibrate or Mute.

1. From the ⏰ Clock menu select ⋮ More options > Settings.

2. To turn this feature on, select Silence when system sound is turned off.

Chapter Five
Contacts

From the Contacts application, you can manage contacts that are stored on your device. You can also synchronize contacts with the Gmail account on your device.

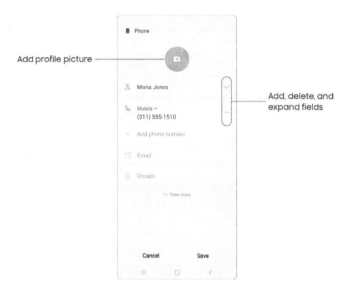

Adding new contacts

1. From the Apps screen, launch Contact application and click + create contact.

2. Enter correctly the details of the contact and click Save.

Editing contacts information

When a contact is being edited you add, edit or remove information. To the contact list of fields new fields can be added.

1. From the Apps screen, tap 😊 Contact application and then click the ✎ Edit button.

2. Click on any field to enter, edit, or delete information then click Save.

Favorites

Favorite contact can be easily accessed from other app as they are arranged on top of your contact list.

○ While on the Apps screen, tap 😊 Contact application, select a number/contact and click ☆ Favorites.

■ To remove a contact from your favorites list tap ★ Favorites.

Sharing contacts

You can share your contact through various sharing methods and services.

1. Enter 👤 Contact application, select a number/contact and press ⇗ Share.

2. You can decide to share the contact as a text or as a vCard file (VCF).

3. Follow the guidelines after selecting a sharing option.

TIP: To share contact information with friends or family easily, click QR code under ⋮ More options while browsing a contact. The QR code updates automatically when the information box is changed.

Groups

You can manage your contacts easily using groups

Creating a new group

Use group to organize your contact list.

1. On ⊕ Contacts application, select Groups under ☰ Show navigation menu.

2. Fill in the details of the group, after clicking Create group.

- Group name: Name the new group so that you can easily identify it.

- Ringtone: Customize a special ringtone for the new group.

- Upload members: Press Done after selecting the contacts to be added to the new group

3. Press Save after entering the required information's.

Delete or add group contacts

Remove or add new contacts to your group. Remove contacts from a group or add new ones.

1. On ⊖ Contacts application, select Groups under ☰ Show navigation menu then choose a group.

2. Press and hold a contact to be removed and click 🗑 Delete.

- To add a contact, select the contact and after clicking Add member under ✎ Edit. Click **Done** to save you work.

Send a message to a group
Text group participants

1. Tap ⊖ Contacts app, select Groups under ☰ Show navigation menu and press a group.

2. Under the ⋮ More options menu click send message.

Send an email to a group

Through email, you can message group members.

1. Press 👤 Contacts app from the Apps screen, select Groups under ☰ Show navigation menu then choose a group.

2. Press ⋮ More options button and then select Email.

3. Pick contact by touching them or click the checkbox on top of the screen to select all and select Done

- This will only display group members with email address

4. Follow the guidelines after an email address has been selected.

Deleting a group

Delete created group.

1. Tap 👤 Contacts app from the Apps screen, select Groups under ☰ Show navigation menu then click a group.

2. Press More options button and then click 🗑 Delete.

- To delete just the group click Delete group only.

- To delete both the group and the members in it click Delete group and move members to trash.

Merge multiple contacts

Contact can be combined from different source into a single entry of contacts when you connect entries in to a single contact.

1. On 👤 Contacts application, select Manage contacts under ☰ Show navigation menu.

2. Select Merge contacts. All contacts with double name, email and phone numbers will be listed together.

3. Click a contact and select Merge.

Import contacts

You bring contacts into your smartphone as a vCard file.

1. On 👤 Contacts app, select Manage contacts under ☰ Show navigation menu.

2. Follow the command on the screen after tapping Import.

Export contacts
Send contacts from your smartphone vCard files.

1. Tap 👤 Contacts app select Manage contacts under ≡ Show navigation menu.

2. Follow the command on the screen after selecting Export contacts.

Synchronize contacts
Update your contacts information in all of you accounts.

1. Launch 👤 Contacts application from the Apps screen, select Manage contacts under ≡ Show navigation menu.

2. Select Contacts Synchronize.

Deleting contacts
Delete one or more contact from your device

1. While on the contact application, press and hold the contact you want to delete and then tap 🗑 .

Emergency contacts

Emergency numbers can be dialed when the smartphone locked.

- o Click Safety and emergency then tap Emergency contacts under the Settings application.
- Add contacts: Choose contacts to serve as emergency numbers on your device.
- Show on the Lock screen: For easy access in an emergency situation Emergency contacts are shown on the lock screen.

Internet

The Samsung Internet application is a quick and reliable web finder. Discover more web browsing features that will make your browsing experience faster and better.

Browsing tabs

Use Tabs to access different sites at once

- o Launch the Internet app and click New tabs under 1 Tab.

- ▪ To exit a tab, click Close tab under 1 Tab.

Creating a Bookmark

Bookmark favorite sites for easy access.

o   On the ⬤ Internet, select ☆ Add to Bookmark to save currently visited sites.

Opening a Bookmark

Use the Bookmark page to open website immediately.

1.   Select ☆ Bookmark while on the Internet page and then tap a Bookmark entry.

Save a webpage

There are numerous ways to save a website in the Samsung Internet app.

o   From the ⬤ Internet app, press ≡ Tools > Add page to access the following choices:

▪   Bookmarks: Save a website to your favorite list.

▪   Quick access: For easy access view a collection of frequently visited webpage.

▪   Home screen: Upload to your Home screen a Website shortcut.

- Saved pages: Save pages to your device so you can access them when you are offline.

View history

o On the Samsung Internet app, click ☰ Tools > History to see a list of recently visited websites.

TIP: To delete all your browsing history, click ⋮ More options > Clear history.

Share pages
Web pages can be shared with friends.

o Launch the Samsung Internet app and follow the guideline after selecting ☰ Tools > Share.

Secret Mode
The browser history or search history do not display the web sites viewed in secret mode, and traces like cookies are not left on your device. The Secret tab color is different from the normal tab color.

Downloaded documents will still remain on your device when you shut the Secret mode down.

1. Launch the Samsung Internet application and tap 🔲 Tabs > Turn on Secret mode.

2. To activate the Secret mode browser select Start.

Settings for Secret Mode

A biometric lock or password is required for the secret mode to be used.

1. On the Samsung Internet, click 1️⃣ Tabs.

2. Tap ⋮ More options> Secret mode settings to select the following settings:

- Password Usage: Create a password to enable Secret mode and use biometric.

- Reset Secret Mode: Delete your Secret mode data and restore defaults.

Deactivate Secret Mode

To browse in standard mode, you have to deactivate Secret Mode.

o From the Samsung Internet app, select 1️⃣ Tabs > Turn off Secret mode.

Messages

Keep in touch with family and friends using the message app to say hello, send emoji and photos.

o From the Samsung Message app, click Compose.

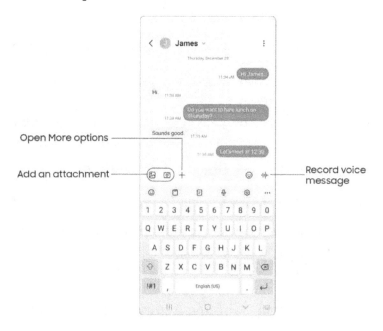

Message search

Find messages quickly using the search feature.

1. On the Samsung Messages app, click the Search button.

2. Type in a few words on the search bar and press the 🔍 search key on the keyboard.

Delete conversation

You can get rid of conversation history by deleting chats.

1. Launch the Samsung Messages app 💬, and click Delete under ⋮ More options.

2. Click on the conversation you wish to delete and then tap the 🗑 Delete button.

Emergency message

Send a message containing images and audio to your emergency number.

o From your Samsung Settings, select 🔒 Safety and emergencies > Emergency SOS. The following actions will pop-up if you press the side key five times:

▪ Countdown range: Select countdown range to begin the emergency steps.

- Place an emergency call: Choose a number to use.

- Share details with emergency contacts: Give them details of your where about.

TIP: Emergency SOS can also be enabled by holding down the Side and Volume Down keys while selecting 📞 Emergency Call.

Emergency sharing

Send your emergency contacts a message that includes images and audio.

1. From your Samsung Settings, select 🔒 Safety and emergency > Emergency Sharing. Select what you want the device to automatically send to your emergency contact:

- Add images: Capture and transmit pictures using your front and back cameras.

- Add audio record: Send to your emergency number a five-second audio recording that is added.

2. Click Begin Emergency sharing to share the media you have chosen to your emergency contact.

Settings for messages

Compose the text and multimedia message settings.

○ Launch the ⬤ Messages program and click ⋮ More options > Settings.

Emergency alerts

Emergency alerts warn you about dangers and other emergencies. It is free to receive an emergency alert.

○ Launch the Samsung Settings application and tap ⬤ Safety and emergency > Wireless Emergency Alerts to personalize alert notification.

TIP: You can view emergency alerts from the notifications panel. Tap ⬤ Notifications > Advanced settings > Wireless Emergency Alerts from the setting application.

My Files

Manage and arrange all your music, videos, photos that are stored on your device. You can manage and access data stored on your cloud account.

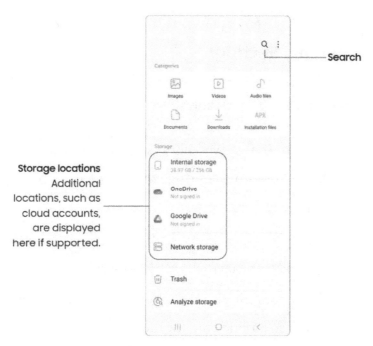

Search

Storage locations
Additional locations, such as cloud accounts, are displayed here if supported.

File groups

File can be grouped into the following category:

- Click Recent Files to access files that you have recently viewed.

  - The following option will appear if one or more files have been recently accessed.

- Categories: Sort files according to type.

- Storage: Access your computer and cloud data.

  - Cloud account varies depending on the kind of service you log in to.

- Check to see what is eating up your storage.

My Files Settings

Use the My File setting feature to change your file management options and more.

o Go to the ⬜ My Files software and select ⋮ More options > Settings to access the following choices:

- Cloud accounts: Log in to your cloud account for easy management of cloud services.

- Managing files: Select how to display, delete, and use mobile data for files.

- Highlight a file size when going through storage

- Privacy: Go through the My File Permission.

Chapter Six
Phone

There are other activities the Phone app can perform apart from making calls. Find out more about the special feature for calling.

Make and Receive Calls

Calls can be made and received through the Phone app on your Home screen, Contacts, Recent tab and more.

Make a call

You can make calls and also receive calls from your Home screen.

- ○ From the 🅲 Phone software, enter a number on the keypad of numbers and click 📞 call.
- ▪ Select Keypad if the keypad does not show.

Make a call from Recents

All calls including the incoming calls, outgoing calls and missed calls are all recorded in the call log.

1. To view your recent calls, click Recent from the 🅲 Phone software.

2. Click a number and touch 📞 Call.

Place a call from Contacts

Calls can be made from your Contacts application.

- ○ While on the 👤 Contact application, swipe your fingers across a contact to place a call.

Receive a Call

You will see the name of a caller when a call comes in and the phone rings. If you are using a program the screen will display and incoming call pop-up.

o To answer a call, swipe the answer button to the right.

TIP: To answer a call when using an application, touch the Answer icon pop-up screen.

Decline a Call

You can decide not to answer an incoming call.

o To reject the incoming call and send it to voicemail, swipe the decline button to the left-hand side.

TIP: Click the decline button on the pop-up screen to reject the call and send it to voicemail.

Reject a Call and Send a Message

o To end a call and leave a message drag upward and select a message from the incoming call screen.

TIP: From the incoming call pop-up screen click Send message and select a message to send.

End a call

If you don't want to answer an incoming call, press End button .

Actions while on a Call

You can multitask, adjust volume and switch to a headset or speaker while on a call. Volumes can be increased or decreased using the volume button.

How to switch to headset or speaker

Bluetooth Speaker or Headset can be used to answer calls.

o   Press ◁)) to listen to the caller on loud speaker or Press ✳ while connected to a Bluetooth headset.

Multitask

If you exit the call screen to use another software or application, your ongoing call will appear on the status bar.

Pull down the status bar to display the notification panel then touch the call to return to it. To end the call, swipe downward to access the notification panel and then press the ⬤ End button.

Call background

Select a video or picture to appear when you make or receive calls.

- o Click Settings> Call background under⋮ More options to access the following features:
- ▪ Layout: You can determine how to display a caller details that has a profile photo.
- ▪ Background: While on a call determine the image to appear.

Settings for Call pop-up

While another app is being used all calls might appear as a pop-up.

- o Click Settings > Call display under⋮ More options while using applications from the 🌀 Phone program. Below are the following options:
- ▪ Full screen: Set the device to show an incoming call in the full screen.
- ▪ Small pop-up: On top of your screen will appear a pop-up notification of an incoming call.

- Mini pop-up: When there is an incoming call display a smaller pop-up.

- Keep calls in pop-up: To keep call in the pop-up view after they have been answered activates this feature.

Call Log

Your calls whether missed, dialed or received are store in your call log from where you can set speed dials, block numbers and use voicemails.

o Launch the Phone app and click Recent. There is a list of recent calls. The caller name appears if they are in you Contacts list.

Save a contact from the list of recent calls

Use the information on your contact list to update you Contacts list of create a new contact

1. Launch the Phone software and click Recent.

2. Click the number you want to save and click Add to contacts.

3. Click Create new contact or Update Existing Contact.

Delete the entire call log

In order to remove Call log entries:

1. Launch your 🅒 Phone software and click Recent.

2. Click the call you want to remove from the call log and tap 🗑 Delete.

Block a number

Call from a blocked call will not be received and they will be sent to your voicemail directly

1. On your 🅒 Phone program, click Recent.

2. Click the caller you want to add to Block list and tap ⓘ Details.

3. Click on ⃠ Block or ⋮ More options > Block contact.

4. Touch OK.

TIP: Your Block list can be modified from Setting by touching More options > Settings> Block numbers from the phone menu.

Speed dial

You can a number a shortcut for easy dialing.

1. On your Phone App, select Keypad > More options > Speed dial numbers. On the speed dial screen will appear the reserved speed dial number

2. Choose a number.

    NOTE: The number 1 is reserved for voicemail; To select another speed dial number from the one that is next in line, click Menu.

3. To set a speed dial number for a contact, type in the details of the contact or tap Add from contacts.

- The selected contact will appear on the speed dial box.

Make a call with Speed Dial

You can make a call using the speed dial.

o Launch the Phone app and press and hold the speed dial number.

- Hold the last digit of the speed dial number after entering it first digit, if the speed dial number has more than one digit.

Delete a Speed dial number

You can also delete Speed dial numbers.

1. Launch the ⓒ Phone software, click ⁝ More options and then tap Speed dial numbers.

2. Select on the number you wish to delete from the speed dial menu and then tap ▬ Delete.

Emergency calls

Call of emergency can be placed to emergency numbers regardless of your network connection. Only this type of call can be made without network connection.

1. Unlock the device and launch the ⓒ Phone app then enter an emergency number like 911 which is used in the North America then tap call.

2. Complete your call. Most in-call capabilities are available to you during this kind of call.

TIP: Someone can call for help by dialing an emergency number even when your device is locked.

149

When accessed from the lock screen only the emergency calling feature is accessible while the remaining features of the device remains locked.

Phone settings

With these options below you can customize the Phone app.

o For Phone app personalization, click Settings under ⋮ More options on the Phone app.

Place a multi-party call

Other calls can be made while a call is ongoing.

1. To make a call with two or more persons, press ✛ Add call from the ongoing call menu.

2. Input the new number and click 📞 Call. When the call has been answered.

- Tap the On-Hold number or press ⮌ Swap to switch between the two calls.

- Press ⤳ Merge to listen to both caller at the same time.

Video calls

Enter a number on the number keypad and press

 Video Call, or ⬭ Video Call to place a Call.

NOTE: Not all gadgets can make video calls. The caller can choose to answer the call as a conventional voice call or accept the video call.

Video call effects

While on a video call you can blur or change the background in various applications.

1. Launch the Settings app on your device and click Video call effects under ⚙ Advanced features.

2. Click ◗ to activate this feature.

3. Choose from the available options:

-   Background Color: Change the virtual color of the background to a solid color depending on your environment.

-   Background image: Select a background photo from the ones on your device.

151

Wi-Fi calling

Calls can be made via Wi-Fi when you log in to a network.

1. Launch the 🅒 Phone Menu and click ⋮ More options and click Wi-Fi calling under Settings.

2. Click ⬤ to activate this feature.

Real Time Text (RTT)

When on an active call, you can share real-time typing with the others.

RTT feature can be used anytime if the device of the person you are call supports RTT or it is connected to a Teletypewriter (TTY) device. On the RTT incoming call screen the RTT icon will pop-up.

1. Launch the 🅒 Phone software and select ⋮ More options > Settings.

2. To use the following Feature press RTT.

■ Button for RTT call: Select the visibility settings for the RTT call button

– Visible during calls: You will see the RTT call button only while on a call.

- Always Visible: Display on the keypad the RTT call button while on a call
- Utilize an external TTY keyboard: Hide the RTT keyboard when an external TTY keyboard is connected
- TTY mode: Choose the Currently used keyboard ideal TTY settings.

Samsung Health

With the Samsung Health software, you can manage your daily routine such as exercise, food and sleep.

NOTE: Details gotten from Samsung Health software is not meant to diagnose, treat, prevent or mitigate illness or other issues.

Your environment might affect the data and information accuracy provided by this device and it associated software, an exacting routine done while wearing the device, the device settings, user configuration and information provided by the user, and other end-user connections.

Before Starting an Exercise Routine

We strongly advice that you see your doctor before you start any work out even though Samsung Health program is a useful fitness partner. See your doctor in the following conditions: disease of the heart, asthma, disease in the lungs, diabetes, diseases in the liver, diseases in the kidney, or arthritis.

Don't forget to call your doctor if you experience any of these symptoms of illness such as pain or discomfort during physical activity in your chest, neck, jaw, or arms.

- Swelling ankles especially in the night
- Consciousness loss or dizziness
- Breath shortness with a little rest or activity
- A fast or noticeable heartbeat
- Muscle soreness that relieves you after taking a reset when climbing stairs or a hill.

Don't start any exercise if you are pregnant, you are unsure of your health or you have several health issues without consulting your doctor.

Samsung Notes

Use the Note software to compose notes. You can create notes with voice recordings, images and more.

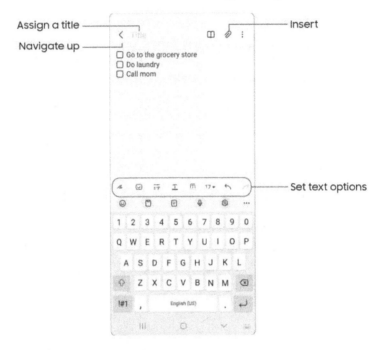

Assign a title

Navigate up

Insert

Set text options

Create notes

Upload Audio files, images and other medial files.

1. Launch the Note Software and click Add notes.

2. Use the text option to create contents.

Voice recordings

In case you are in a meeting or seminar use voice recording to take notes.

1. From the 🔲 Note program, click ⓔ Add.

2. Click 📎 Insert and touch voice recording.

3. Create content while recording audio.

Edit notes

Edit to your written notes.

1. Select a note to view in the Note app and then tap 🖉 Edit.

2. Click ‹ Back button to save correction.

Notes options

You can arrange, manage and personalize notes. From the Samsung notes program, you will find the following:

○ Launch the 🔲 Notes application.

▪ 📄+ Import PDF: Launch a PDF file in Notes app.

- 🔍 Search: Press the Search button and enter a key work.

- ⋮ Other options:

  - Edit: Select the Note you want to share edit or delete.

  - View: Select from the Grid, List, or Simple list choices.

  - Pin your Favorite note to top: Notes that are mark as favorite are stored at the top of the main page.

Notes Menu

By category your notes can be accessed.

- o To use the following options, click ▤ Show Navigation Menu under Samsung Notes:

- ⚙ Settings: Use the settings for the Samsung Notes app.

- All notes: View your created notes

- Notes Shared: View shares notes with your Samsung accounts.

- View notes that have been trashed for up to 15 days.
- Folders: Sort notes into folders.
- Manage folders: Folders can be deleted, created and edited.

Settings
Access Settings

The Settings on your devices can be accessed through several ways.

- Choose ⚙ Settings from the Notification panel.

- Choose ⚙ Settings from the Apps panel.

Search for settings

Search for a setting that you can't really find.

1. On the Settings, click 🔍 and input a word.

2. Click on an entry to access the setting.

Chapter Seven
Connections

With connection you can control the network between your device and other devices or networks.

Wi-Fi

Connect your device to a Wi-Fi network to access the internet without mobile data.

1. Launch the Settings app on your device and click Connections>Wi-Fi.

2. Click to enable Wi-Fi and search for more networks.

3. Select a network and enter it password.

4. Press Connect to join the network.

Connect to a hidden Wi-Fi network

Enter the Wi-Fi network details manually when the network refuses to appear after performing a deep scan. Before you begin ask the network administrator for the name and password of the network.

1. Launch the Settings app and click Wi-Fi under connections then tap to turn on Wi-Fi.

161

2. Click ✛ Add network under the list

3. Enter the Wi-Fi network details:

- Network name: Under here enter the full name of the network.

- Security: From the list of security options select one, and input password if necessary.

- Password: Enter the password of the network.

- View more: Indicate other stylish settings, like IP and proxy settings.

4. Touch Save.

TIP: To join a network, use the camera to scan the QR code.

Wi-Fi Direct

You can transfer data over Wi-Fi using the Wi-Fi direct feature.

1. Launch the Settings application, click Wi-Fi under 📶 Connections and then click ⬤ to turn on Wi-Fi.

2. Under the ⋮ More options, click Wi-Fi Direct.

3. Follow the instruction after selecting a device to connect to.

Disconnect from Wi-Fi Direct

Disconnect your device from a Wi-Fi direct.

o To access Wi-Fi Direct, launch the Settings application, click 🛜 Connections > Wi-Fi > ⋮ More option > Wi-Fi Direct. Click a device disengage it.

Intelligent Wi-Fi Settings

Under this menu, you can be able to check up your device, control saved networks and personalize connections to various Wi-Fi networks.

1. Launch the Settings application, click Wi-Fi under 🛜 Connections and then press ⬤ to turn on Wi-Fi.

2. To see the following options, click ⋮ More options and select Intelligent Wi-Fi:

▪ Switch to mobile data: The mobile device uses your data to operate whenever the Wi-Fi is unstable and use Wi-Fi when connection returns.

- Switch to better Wi-Fi network: The device will automatically switch to a stronger Wi-Fi network.

- Turn Wi-Fi on/off automatically: Activate Wi-Fi in frequently visited locations.

- Show network quality info: In the list of networks, show the speed and durability information of the network.

- Prioritize real-time data: Give Games, video calls, and more lag-sensitive task this treatment.

- Detect suspicious networks: When current Wi-Fi network emits suspicious behavior, you will receive an alert.

- Wi-Fi power saving mode: To save battery, enable Wi-Fi traffic in the power saving mode.

- Auto Hotspot connection: Your device will connect to any available network automatically.

Advanced Wi-Fi settings

Under this menu you can be able to check up tour device, control saved networks and personalize connections to various Wi-Fi networks.

1. Launch the Settings application, click Wi-Fi under ⌢ Connections and then tap ⬭ to turn on Wi-Fi.

2. Touch ⁝ More options and then press Advanced configurations for the following options:

- Sync Samsung Cloud/Account: Your profile of Wi-Fi will be synced with your Samsung account automatically.

- Display Pop-up for Wi-Fi: Receive a notification that Wi-Fi is available when accessing an app.

- Wi-Fi and network notification: Receive a notification when close by devices are detected.

- Control networks: Choose the network you want to reconnect of forget under the list of saved networks.

- Wi-Fi on/off history: View the frequent use of Wi-Fi as well as usage by apps.

- Hotspot 2.0: Automatically connect to Wi-Fi networks that support Hotspot 2.0.

Bluetooth

Use your device to connect other Bluetooth supported devices such as Bluetooth speakers and more. You will not need to enter passkey again if you have connected device before because they will remember each other.

1. Launch the Settings program, click Bluetooth under 🛜 Connections and then tap ⬤ to turn on Wi-Fi.

2. Click a device.

TIP: Press 🔵 Bluetooth when sharing a file.

Rename a paired device

You can rename a paired device for it to be easy to recognize.

1. Unlock the device, click 🛜 Connections > Bluetooth and then click ⬤ to enable Bluetooth.

2. Press ⚙️ Settings next to the device name.

3. Click Rename and then enter the new name.

Un-pair from a Bluetooth device

If devices have been un-paired, they will no longer remember each other and you will need a passcode to connect it again.

1. Unlock the device, click 🛜 Connections > Bluetooth and then click ⬤ to enable Bluetooth.

2. Click ⚙ Settings next to the device.

3. Click Un-pair.

Advanced Bluetooth Settings

More Bluetooth features can be accessed from the Advanced menu.

1. Unlock the device and click 🛜 Connections > Bluetooth.

2. Tap Advanced settings or More ⋮ options > Advanced settings to access the following features:

- Synchronize with Samsung Cloud: Synchronize files transferred via Bluetooth with your Samsung account or the Samsung Cloud.

- Music Sharing: You can give friends the permission to listen to songs using your Bluetooth speaker or headphone.

- Ringtone Synchronize: When a call is received via a connected Bluetooth device, use the ringtone that is configured on the device.

- Bluetooth control history: View how often you use Bluetooth feature.

- Block pairing requests: You can add device to block pairing requests.

Dual Audio

With dual audio feature, you can play audio from your device to two other different connected Bluetooth devices.

1. Create a pairing between your device and other audio devices.

2. Pull down the notification panel and select media output.

3. Press the button ✅ next to each audio device to play audio to them.

NFC and Payment

With the Near Field Communication, you can communicate with other devices without a network connection. You can also make payment using the NFC feature. When using this feature, make sure both devices are within four centimeters away.

o Click Settings > 📶 Connections > NFC and contactless payments. To activate this feature on your Smartphone, tap 🔘.

Tap and pay

Payments can be done when you merge your device to the NFC credit card reader.

1. Click Settings > 📶 Connections > NFC and contactless payments. To activate this feature on your Smartphone, tap 🔘.

2. Click contactless payments to view the payment application.

- If you want to use another payment app to select another payment for apps.

- To use an app that is open to make payment click Pay with currently open app.

- To use another app for payment, select Others.

Ultra-wideband

Detect the exact location of nearby devices.

○ Launch Settings > Connection > Ultra-Wide Band. To activate it on your Smartphone, tap .

Airplane Mode

All connectivity will go off once the airplane mode is turned on. You can on Wi-Fi or Bluetooth while airplane mode is on from Quick settings.

○ Click Settings > Connection > Airplane mode. To activate this feature on your Smartphone, tap .

NOTE: Using mobile phones on Ships and Airplanes is not supported by the Federal and local rules. Activate Airplane mode to deactivate all connectivity.

Activate the Airplane mode to deactivate the Ultra-Wideband feature, which is not allowed on vehicles or ships. Consult right authorities for the right time to use your device.

SIM Management

Your service provider can allow the usage of dual SIM (two physical SIM) or an eSIM (fixed SIM card) in order to control two accounts without carrying the devices. The option varies depending on provider of service.

Device that can use dual SIM has two slots. A microSD card might be included if supported. Device that can use Dual SIM will receive software upgrades after launch that enables the built-in-feature.

Without a real SIM you can use your eSIM on supported devices. This action turns on voice, text, and data to be utilized with either the eSIM or the supportive SIM card. After open, updates on software that enable the integrated eSIM feature will be shared to devices that support eSIM.

o Click Settings > Connections > SIM Management to access the following:

- SIM card: From your Smart phone View installed physical SIM cards, you can change their names, turn them on or off.

- eSIMs: To include an existing eSIM mobile plan or sign up for new ones, click Add eSIM.

- Primary SIM: Set up a primary card that will be used for calls and other media if you have more than one SIM card.

- More SIM settings: Click this option to find out more SIM card management options.

Mobile networks

With this feature, you can personalize your device to connect to mobile networks and have access or use mobile data.

o Launch Settings > Connections and then tap Mobile networks to activate the feature.

- Mobile data: Permit mobile data usage.

- International data roaming: You can change settings for voice, text, and data roaming for international roaming.
- Data roaming access: While roaming for data personalize access to mobile networks.
- Data roaming: Permit data usage while you are travelling across mobile networks.
- Enhanced Calling feature: Activate the enhanced communication with LTE.
- System selection: You can switch to the CDMA roaming mode if it is supported by your service provider.
- Access Point Names (APNs): The APNs are the requirements your device needs to connect its service provider; choose or add APNs.
- Network manager: Choose your preferred network.
- Mobile networks Diagnostics: Gather use and diagnostic details for troubleshooting.

TIP: Use this option to control connection settings that may have an impact on your monthly payment.

Data Usage

Check your current data and Wi-Fi usage. You can set up limitation and warnings.

o Launch Settings app on the device > Connections > Data consumption.

Switch on Data Saver

You can activate the data saving feature to block specific apps from sending and receiving data in the background.

1. Launch Settings app on the device > Connections >Data consumption.

2. Select this icon to activate data saver.

- To use data while data saver is on, click allow and then if you want to limit some apps from consuming data, press next to each application.

Monitor Mobile Data

By putting constraints and controls in place, you may personalize your mobile data access.

o Launch Settings application on your device > Connections > Data consumption. The following options will appear:

- Mobile data: Use mobile data from your package.

- International data roaming: Allow data while roaming internationally.

- Apps that can use mobile data: Select applications that will use data even when your device is connected to a Wi-Fi network.

- Mobile data usage: While connected to a mobile device over a period of time check the amount of data used, both total usage and usage broken down per app.

- Billing cycle and data warning: Change the monthly date to correspond with the billing date that your service provider has configured.

Monitor Wi-Fi Data

You can restrict Wi-Fi data usage by personalizing usage caps and networks to your specifications.

1. Click Settings on your smartphone > Connection > Data usage.

2. Click Wi-Fi data usage to track your data over Wi-Fi connections. Both total usage and usage broken down by apps are available.

Mobile Hotspot

With the mobile Hotspot many devices can connect to your mobile data.

1. Unlock the device, click Settings > Connections > Mobile hotspot and then tap Tethering.

2. Press ⬤ to switch on mobile hotspot

3. Enable Wi-Fi on the devices you want to connect to, select your mobile hotspot option, and then enter the password.

• Under connected device you will find the list of devices you have connected to.

TIP: You can scan QR code instead of entering password.

Set up mobile hotspot settings

Change your hotspot connectivity and security option.

1. Unlock the device, click Settings > 🛜 Connections > Mobile hotspot and tap Tethering.

2. To use the following, click configure:

- Network Name: See and change your mobile hotspot name.

- Band: Select from the list of bandwidth options.

- Security: Choose the level of your Hotspot security.

- Advanced: Configure more hotspot settings.

Auto hotspot

With this feature sharing your mobile hotspot to other devices that are signed in to your Samsung account is very easy.

1. Unlock the device, click Settings > 🛜 Connections > Mobile hotspot > Tethering and tap Mobile hotspot.

2. Click Auto hotspot and click ⬭ to activate this feature.

Tethering

Tethering allows you to connect another device to your device's Internet connection.

1. Unlock the device, click Settings > 📶 Connections > Mobile hotspot and tap Tethering.

2. Choose from the list of options:

- To share your device's internet connection with Bluetooth, click Bluetooth tethering.

- To share your device's internet connection via USB, click USB tethering.

- To share your device's internet connection via an Ethernet cable, click Ethernet tethering.

Scanning Nearby Device

You can quickly connect to another available device's when you turn on the Nearby device Scanning. You will get a notification when there are devices to connect to.

1. Select settings on your mobile device, click on Connections > More connection settings > Nearby device scanning.

2. To turn on this feature, click .

Ethernet

Your device can be connected to a local network via an Ethernet cable, if a wireless network connection is unavailable.

1. Plugin an Ethernet Cord to your device.

2. Click Settings on your mobile device, click Connection >, More connection setting > Ethernet.

TIP: An adapter is needed to connect your device to an Ethernet cable.

Network lock status

View your device's network status lock to see if it can be unlocked for another network to use.

o Launch the Settings on your smartphone, click Connections > More connection settings > Network local status.

Connected devices

You can achieve mobile continuity between your device and other devices. Click Connected device under settings to view the following options:

- Fast Share: Share file between your device and anyone that has a Samsung account.

- Switch Buds Automatically: Your Galaxy Bud will automatically switch from another device to yours when you make a call or play media

- From other device Call and text: With the Galaxy device logged into your Samsung account you can place and receive calls and also text messages.

- Continue apps usage on other devices: You can continue from you left on your Smartphone on Galaxy device that are logged in to your Samsung account.

- Link to Windows: Create a connection between a window PC and your Smartphone to have access to your device images, message and videos.

- Multi controls: Use your Galaxy keyboard and the cursor on the Galaxy book to move items on your device.

- Samsung DeX: Connect your device to a PC or TV for a better experience in multitasking.

- Smart View: Show the current screen of your smartphone on a nearby TV.

- Galaxy Wearable: Connect your ear bud to your Samsung Galaxy watch.

- SmartThings: Connect to a location of smarter living solutions.

- Android Auto: For you to concentrate while driving connect your device with any compatible car display.

Sound and Vibration

You can control your system sound and other interaction on your device.

Sound mode

In absence of the volume control you can still change your device sound.

○ Click Settings on your smartphone and then click Sound & Vibration to select a mode:

▪ Sound: Use the sound, vibrations and volume levels you selected from the sound settings for notifications and alerts.

− Vibrate while ringing: Set your phone to vibrate alongside ringing when you receive a call.

▪ Vibrate: Vibrate only for alerts and notifications.

▪ Mute: Deactivate all sound output on your Smartphone

− Mute temporarily: Determine the time frame for your device to be muted.

TIP Instead of using volume key, use the sound settings to change the sound mode without wiping away your personalized sound settings.

Mute with gestures

Cover the screen of your smartphone to quickly mute sound.

o Click Settings on your smartphone, press Advanced options > Motion & gestures > Mute with gestures and then click to make the feature active.

Vibrations

You can control your device vibration.

1. Launch the Settings and click Sound & Vibration.

2. Click a customizable option:

- Call vibration: Choose from default vibration patterns.

- Notification Vibration: Choose from default vibration patterns.

- System vibration: For the following options set the vibration amplitude and feedback.

- Vibration intensity: Move the slider to change the vibration intensity.
- Touch interaction: You will notice a vibration on your device when you tap the navigation buttons or press and hold objects on the screen.
- Dialing keypad: When typing numbers, the keypad will vibrate.
- Samsung keyboard: The Samsung keyboard will vibrate when it's in use.
- Charging: Device will vibrate when charging.
- Navigation gestures: When using gestures device will vibrate.
- Camera: The device will vibrate when capturing pictures.
- Vibration intensity: To personalize the vibration pattern for call and notifications and touch interactions drag the vibration slider.

Volume

Configure volume levels for calls ringtone, media and notifications.

o Launch your smartphone Settings app and select Volume under 🔊 Sound & vibration.

TIP: Volume levels can be adjusted using the volume keys. When you press the volume the volume level will appear on the screen. Move the slider up or down to change the sound level.

Use Volume keys for Media

Use the volume key to customize your media sound system instead of using the currently playing sound.

1. Launch your smartphone Settings and click Volume under 🔊 Sound & vibration.

2. Click **Use volume key for media** to make the feature active.

Media Volume Limit

Set a maximum output of volume at a reasonable level when using Bluetooth speakers or headphones.

1. From your smartphone Settings and click Volume under 🔊 Sound & vibration menu.

2. Under ⋮ More options click on Media volume limit.

3. Click on this icon ⬤ to activate this feature.

- To select the highest possible volume output, move the custom volume slider.

- To protect your volume password click Set volume limit PIN.

Ringtone

You can customize your personal ringtone or select from system ringtones.

1. Go to Settings, select 🔊 Sound & vibration and then click Ringtone.

2. Move the slider to change the ringtone volume.

3. Click ✛ Add or select a ringtone from your device to use it as a ringtone.

Notification Sound

Choose from your device a preloaded notification alert sound.

1. Launch your settings app, click 🔊 Sound & vibrations and touch Notifications.

2. Move the slider to change the notification sound volume.

3. Click on a sound to hear a quick preview of it.

TIP: You can allocate a notification sound to each app from the App Settings.

Notifications

Streamline apps notifications can be prioritized by selecting which application send notification and how you are notified.

Application notifications

Choose apps to send notifications.

- o Select Settings > ⬤ Notifications > App notifications to activate notifications for specific apps.

Lock screen notification

Choose notification to appear on the lock screen.

- o Click Settings > ⬤ Notifications > Lock screen notifications. To activate this feature, press ⬤ and then pick an option to personalize:

- ▪ Don't Show contents: Notifications in the notification panel will appear.

- Show content: Notifications will appear in the notification section.

- Display content when unlocked: Show contents on notification when device is unlocked.

- Notifications to appear: Pick the notifications you want to appear on the Lock screen.

- Display on Always On Display: Show notifications on the Always on Display screen.

Notification pop-up pattern

You can change the pop-up pattern for notification and other options.

o From your Settings > tap Notifications > Notification pop-up style and then select a pop-up pattern.

- Brief: Configure your notifications to be editable.

- Apps to display as brief: Choose app to appear as brief notifications.

- Edge lighting design: Select notification edge lightning design.

- Color by keyword: For notifications that contain important details custom colors can be selected.

- Appear when your screen is not on: Determine whether to show notifications or not when your screen is not on.

• Detailed: Personalize Samsung Default notification setting.

Do Not Disturb

With this feature you can block sound and notifications. You can set exception for application, calls and alerts.

o From Settings app of your smartphone, press Notification > Do Not Disturb and set up the following.

• Do not disturb: To deactivate all notification and sound, activate Do Not Disturb.

• How much time? Select a time frame for Do not disturb when you activate it manually.

Schedule

- Sleeping: Set a time for Do Not Disturb to automatically turn on.

- Include a schedule: Configure a new routine to indicate the days and times at which your smartphone will typically be in Do not disturb mode.

Allow while Do Not Disturb in on

- Calls and messages: Allow calls and messages while Do Not Disturb is activated.

- Apps notifications: Add applications you want to receive their notifications while in Do not Disturb mode. You will receive notification even if all media are blocked.

- Sound and Vibration: Enable Sound and vibrations from alarms and events while this mode is activated.

Advanced Notifications Setting

You can set up notifications from applications and other services.

- o Launch the Settings software and click on Notifications > Advanced options.

- Notification Icons: Allow the notification number to appear on the status bar.
- Show the percentage of battery: The remaining battery life of your Smartphone will appear on the status bar.
- Notification history: Show all received notifications.
- Conversation: View chats alerts in conversations. Press and hold a conversation to silence it.
- Floating notifications: To activate floating alert, select the bubbles or smart pop-up view.
- Suggest emojis and replies for notification: Receive suggestion for right responses to notifications and actions to messages.
- Display snooze button: Allow button that enable you to rapidly ignore notifications to appear.
- Notification Reminders: Enable and personalize frequent notification reminders from certain programs and services. Delete the notification to end the reminder.

- Badges for Apps icon: To see programs that have active notifications use badges that display on app icons. Select whether badges show the quantity of unread alerts or not by clicking it.

- Wireless Emergency Alerts: Customize alert notifications.

Alert when the device is picked up

You can set up your smartphone to alert you about missed calls and messages by vibrating.

o To enable this feature, launch the Settings app and click Advanced option > Motion and gestures > Alert when phone picked up.

Chapter Eight
Display

You can configure your screen display (size, delay and timeout).

Dark mode

Activate dark mode to keep your eyes at rest in the night, you can also make your screen bright in dark mode.

- To access the follow, click Settings >
  Display:
- Light: Configure the color of your smartphone to light.
- Dark: Configure the color theme of your smartphone to be dark.
- Settings for Dark mode: Select where to use dark mode.
- Turn on as scheduled: Configure dark mode for a specific time.

Screen brightness

Modify your screen brightness to match your taste.

1. Go to settings and then press   Display.

2. Customize the brightness options:

- Drag the slider of brightness to change the brightness level.

- To have a screen brightness change depending on the ambient light click Adaptive brightness

- Click Additional brightness to boost the maximum brightness if the Adaptive brightness is turned off.

TIP: From the Quick you can also change the screen brightness.

Motion Smoothness

Increase the refresh rate of your screen for smoother scrolling.

1. Launch your smartphone Settings and click Motion smoothness under Display.

2. Choose an option and click apply.

Eye comfort shield

With this feature, you can sleep better at night. You can set up a schedule to switch this feature on or off automatically.

1. Open the device, go to Settings, tap Display > Eye comfort shield and then click to activate this feature.

2. Choose a customizable option:

- Adaptive: Set to Adaptive so that you can automatically change your screen color temperature depending on your usage patterns and the time.

- Custom: Set to Custom to allow you set up a schedule for when the Eye Comfort Shield should be turned on.

  - Click Set schedule and select Always on, Sunset to sunrise, or Custom.

  - Move the color temperature slider to adjust the opacity filter.

Accidental touch protection

Prevent your screen from identifying touch input when your device is in a dark area like your pocket or bag.

- o Launch your smartphone settings, click Accidental touch protection under Display menu.

Touch Sensitivity

To increase the screen touch sensitivity for use with screen protectors, Go to Settings and hit Display > Touch sensitivity.

Show charging information

The remaining time for your battery to be fully will appear on your screen.

- o Launch your Smartphone Settings, tap Display > Show Charging details.

Screen Saver

Colors and images can appear while charging your device.

1. While on the Settings page, click Screen saver from the Display menu.

2. Choose from the list of options:

- None: Do not show screen saver at all.

- Colors: Choose a selector to bring up a screen with hues that are shifting.

- Photo Table: Display all photos on your photo table.

- Photo frame: Display all photos in the photo frame.

- Photos: From the Photos app, show all image on your Google photos account.

3. To activate the chosen screen saver click preview.

TIP: To utilize the more options click Settings close to the feature.

Lift to Wake

○ To enable this feature, launch Settings > Advanced options > Motion and Gestures > Lift to Wake.

Double tap to turn on screen

o   To activate this feature, launch the settings app, click Advanced options > Motion and gestures > Double tap to turn on screen.

Double tap to turn off screen

o   To activate this feature, launch the settings application, click Advanced options > Motion and gestures > Double tap to turn off screen.

Keep screen on while viewing

Detect your gaze with the front camera to keep your screen on while looking at it.

o   Launch the settings app, click Advanced options > Motion and gestures and then tap Keep your screen on as you watch. Press the activation button to make the feature active.

One-hand Mode

Change the layout of the device screen so you can comfortably operate the device using just one hand.

1. Launch the device Settings, tap ⚙ Advanced Option and then select One-Handed Mode.

2. Pick one of the following after tapping the activation button 🔘.

- Motion: From the center of your screen bottom edge swipe downward.

- Button: Quickly click ⬜ Home twice to reduce the size of display.

Chapter Nine
Lock screen and security

The information on your device is safe when a screen lock is set.

Screen Lock Types

You will only find Pattern, PIN, Password, None and Swipe as the available screen lock.

NOTE: To restrict access to your device and safeguard it content the biometric lock is available on your device.

Set a secure screen lock

It is better to keep your smartphone content safe with Password, PIN, or Pattern, and to set up biometric lock this is also required.

1. Go to Settings > Screen Lock > Lock Screen > Screen Lock Types.

2. Click to make visual alerts on your screen. you will see the following options:

- Don't show content: Notifications will not appear in the notification panel.

- Display content: Notification will appear in the notification panel.

- Display content when unlocked: Notification content will display when the device screen is unlocked.

- Notifications to appear: Set limitations on notifications that appear on the Lock screen.

- Display on Always On Display: Show notification content on the AOD screen.

3. To close the menu, click Done

4. Configure the following screen lock options:

- Smart Lock: When trusted locations or device are found your device will automatically unlock. You need a reliable screen lock for this feature.

- Lock screen: Touch to change what is displaying and how it appears.

- Widgets: To adjust the widget that shows up with clock on the lock screen, tap the widgets.

- Press and hold to edit: Press and hold items to edit them.

- Always On Display: Activate AOD.

- Roaming clock: A moving clock that shows the time both your location.

Find My Mobile

You can safeguard your Smartphone from being stolen by allowing it to be locked, tracked online and have your data remotely wiped.

Turn on Find My Mobile

For you to use the Find My Mobile feature you must enable it first in your device settings. To gain remote access to your smartphone, Visit findmymobile.samsung.com.

1. Launch your Smartphone Settings, tap Security & Privacy > Find My Mobile > tap Allow this device to be found.

2. To activate this feature, click and then sign in to your Samsung account. The following options will appear:

- Allow this Smartphone to be seen: Activate this option to allow easy access to lost phone.

- Remote unlock: To manage and unlock your device from a distance give Samsung the permission to save your screen lock patterns.

- Display latest location: Enable the Galaxy S24 ultra to send it recent location to the Find My Mobile server when the battery drops beyond an estimated level.

Google Play Protect

With Google you can automatically scan your applications and system for security and threats.

o Launch the device Setting > Security & privacy > Apps Security > Google Play Protect.

Security update

You can check your last updated date and also see if there is a new version to upgrade to.

o Launch the device Settings application and click on Security & Privacy > Updates > Security Updates.

Samsung Privacy

Send analytical report to Samsung when your device is having some technical issues.

1. Launch the device Settings application, click on

    Security & privacy > Privacy > Other privacy settings.

2. Click Samsung and select one of the following to personalize:

*   Samsung Privacy: See Samsung Privacy Policy Details.

*   Customization service: Allow Samsung to offer suggestions and details that are tailored to you.

*   Send diagnostic data: Send analytic data to Samsung when your device is facing some technical issues.

Google Privacy

Change the Google privacy settings.

1. Launch the device settings, press Security & privacy > Privacy > Other privacy settings.

2. Click Google to change privacy services.

Samsung Pass

Use the Samsung Pass application to access your desired services using biometric. You must be logged in to your Samsung account to use the Samsung pass feature.

1. Choose Samsung Pass under ⬤ Security & Privacy from the Settings menu.

2. After logging in, add your biometric data to your Samsung Account.

Samsung Blockchain keystore

Control your blockchain private key.

1. Choose Samsung Block Chain Key Store under ⬤ Security & privacy > Samsung blockchain keystore from the Settings menu.

2. To import or create a new crypto wallet, follow the guidelines on the screen.

Install unknown application

You can set your device to install applications from unknown sources.

1. Launch the device Settings. click Install unknown apps under Security & Privacy.

2. To allow installation of apps from unknown sources, click ⬭ .

TIP: Your device and personal data may be exposed to threats by installing apps from unknown sources.

Password for factor data reset

You can require a password from your service provider to restore your device to factory default settings.

- o Launch your device settings application, click 🛡 Security & Privacy > Other Security settings > Set up/change password then enter the passcode.

Set up SIM card lock

You can lock your SIM with a PIN to restrict access if someone tries to use you SIM card.

- o Launch the device settings software, click 🛡 Security & Privacy and then tap other Security Settings > Set up SIM card lock.
- ▪ Click Lock SIM card to turn this feature on.

- To generate a new PIN, tap Change SIM card PIN.

View passwords

You will see password characters briefly as you type.

o Launch the Settings application, click on
Security & Privacy > Other Settings and then
tap Make passwords visible. You need a
password to activate this feature.

Device administration

Administrative access to your device can be granted
to apps and security tools.

1. Launch the Settings Program, click Security
and Privacy > Other Security Settings > Device
admin application.

2. Click an option to activate it as a device
administrator.

Credentials Storage

You can manage the smartphone's trusted security certificates, which confirm legitimacy of server for safe connections.

- While on settings page, click Security & Privacy > Other security settings. The options under are available:

- View security certificates: Put security certificates on your device display so they can be viewed.

- User certificates: View the certificate of the user that identify you Smartphone in this section.

- Install from phone storage: Use the device storage option to install a recent certificate from your storage.

- Delete credentials: You can delete the contents on your device credentials and reset password.

- Certificate management application: Pick a certificate management application to manage the contents of your certificates.

Location

Location services using a combination of GPS, a mobile network and Wi-Fi determines the location of your device.

1. Launch the Settings app on your smartphone and click Location.

2. To turn location services on, tap the activation button .

TIP: You must turn location on in order for some programs to function.

Application permissions

Applications that require access to your location service can be given permission.

1. Launch the settings application and click Apps permission under Location.

2. Tap an app to grant it permission. Each app has their own option.

Location services

Your location service stores and uses the most recent location data. To improve your search result based on places that you recently visited, some apps may use this detail.

1. Under the Settings Menu, click Location.

2. Click an entry under Location to view see the way your location information is used.

Improve accuracy

You can enable other location scanning tools.

1. Under Settings, click Location and then tap Location services.

2. Click a connection method under improved accuracy to add or remove it for location service.

- Scan Wi-Fi: Even when the Wi-Fi is off you can activate automatic Wi-Fi network scanning for apps.

- Scan Bluetooth: Even when Bluetooth is off you can enable apps to search and connect to nearby devices.

Recent access

View the list of apps that have recently asked for your location.

1. Launch the Settings menu and click Location.

2. To turn on this feature, tap the activation button .

3. To reveal the settings for an application, press an entry under Recent access option.

Emergency location services

Your device may automatically broadcast its location to emergency response partners when you type or text an emergency number if your area supports Emergency Location Service (ELS).

1. Under Settings, click Safety and emergency > Emergency Location service.

2. Click the activation button to enable Emergency location service.

Chapter Ten
Accounts

All account including your Samsung account, Google account and social networking can be managed.

Add an account

You can add and sync all your emails, social networking and file sharing account.

1. Launch Settings > ⟳ Accounts and Backup > Manage account > ＋ Add account.

2. Choose a type of account.

3. Follow the guideline on the screen to enter your login details and create account.

- Click Auto sync data to allow automatic updates to your accounts.

Account settings

All accounts have their own settings. All accounts of the same type might have common setup.

1. Launch the Settings program and then click ⟳ Account & Backup > Manage Account.

2. To change a profile setting, click on it.

Remove an account

1. Launch the Settings program and then click ![icon] Account and Backup > Manage Account.

2. Click Remove after selecting the account you want to delete.

Backup and Restore

Your phone can backup data to personal account.

Samsung account

You can enable data backup to your Samsung account.

o Enter Settings > ![icon] Account & Backup > Samsung Cloud and then select one of the following:

▪ Backup Data: On your Samsung Account, set up data backup.

▪ Data Restore: Sign in to your account to restore data backup.

Google Account

You can turn on data backup on your Google account.

1. From Settings, click ![icon] Account and Backup.

2. On the Google drive menu tap Backup data.

Move to External Storage

With the USB storage device or the Smart Switch, you can backup data to your device.

- o Launch the Settings app > Account & Backup > External Storage Transfer.

Google settings

You can modify your Google account settings. Google account will determine the settings to be available.

- o Click Settings > Google, select a custom setting.

Date & Time

Time and Date can be obtained from wireless network. You can also set time and date manually if there is no network coverage.

- o Launch Setting program, click General Management and then tap Time and Date. The options under are available:
- Automatic Time and Date: You will receive date and time update from your wireless network.

You can select from the following options when automatic date and time is disabled:

- Set date: Enter Current day to set date.
- Set time: Enter the current Time.
- Automatic time zone: Use your network provided time zone.
- Choose a different time zone
- Change time zone depending on your location: Receive time update depending on your area.
- Use 24-hour format: Select the display format of time.

Reset

Reset network and device settings. You can also restore the factory defaults on your device.

Reset every setting

Everything on your device can be restored to factory defaults, except from security, language, and account settings. Personal details remain intact.

1. Launch the Settings application, select General Management > Reset > Reset all Settings.

2. Click Yes when asked after selecting Reset Settings.

Reset network settings

Wi-Fi, and Bluetooth settings will be cleared when you reset network settings.

1. Tap General management > Reset > Reset network settings from the Settings menu.

2. Select Reset settings, and then click Yes when asked.

Reset accessibility settings

You can reset device accessibility. Your downloaded applications and personal details remain intact.

1. Launch the Settings application > General Management > Reset > Reset accessibility Settings.

2. Select Reset settings, and then click Yes when asked.

Reset Factory Data

By Setting your device to factory default, all the data on your device will be deleted.

All media, applications and accounts on your device will be deleted once this is done.

Once a lock screen is activated when you log in to a Google account, Google Device Protection will activate automatically.

NOTE: it will take up to 24 hours for your new password to link with all accounts connected devices if the password was changed.

Before proceeding on resetting your device:

1. Ensure you transfer your important data to your external storage.

2. Double check your login details by signing in to your Google account.

How to reset your device:

1. Launch the Settings Program and click Factory data reset under Reset from the General Management menu.

2. Click Reset and follow the on-screen commands to begin reset.

3. Follow the instructions on the screen to setup your mobile device after a reset it.